Pre-Publication Notices

In *Monsters in Life and Literature* Dr. Demuth takes the reader on a journey into the world of the forensic psychologist, tasked with understanding the most extreme forms of what is usually referred to as the human capacity for evil. Demuth joins his long experience with the inhabitants of this world with his training as a Jungian psychoanalyst to cast light in the darkness through his theoretical reflections and his detailed examination of monsters found in myth and literature. The book is essential reading for anyone concerned with understanding these regions of darkness in the human condition.

—GEORGE HOGENSON, PH.D.
Senior Training Analyst at the C G Jung Institute
of Chicago and the author of *Jung's Struggle with
Freud—A Metabiological Study*. (2013)

A unique and profoundly written book. Dr. Demuth astutely captures key points regarding the duality of human beings, especially the desired good and the sinister evil in all of us. An outstanding contribution to the field of forensic psychology as well as a resource to the general reader.

—RANDY STARR, Author of *Not Guilty by Reason
of Insanity: One Man's Recovery* (2000). Contact:
rommeldale0@gmail.com

Monsters in Life and Literature is a thought-provoking exploration into the human psyche. It offers the reader a glimpse into the dark and intricate world of forensic evaluation and depth psychology. Dr. Demuth provides invaluable insights into the empathic challenges one faces when confronted with criminality, psychopathy, and yes, ultimate evil. Demuth delves into how the complexities of free will, genetics, social environment, trauma, morality, and conscience, all contribute to different mindsets and behavior.

—VLADO SOLC, Jungian Analyst and co-author of
Dark Religion: Fundamentalism from the Perspective of Jungian Psychology

If your clinical thoughts about psychology conjure images of Dante's *Inferno*, you must read this book. Equally literary and scientific, it is a thought-provoking *tour de force*.

—REID MELOY, PH. D.,
Author of *The Psychopathic Mind*

MONSTERS IN LIFE AND LITERATURE

A Forensic Psychologist Reflects
on the Nature of Good and Evil

Group discounts are available (10 or more copies)
Contact dyane@analyticalpsychologypress.com

Book Design: Dyane Sherwood

Published in 2023
Dancing Raven Press
An imprint of Analytical Psychology Press
502 Lee Street 3E, Evanston, IL 60202-1883, United States

https://analyticalpsychologypress.com

ISBN: 978-1-958263-09-9 paperback
ISBN: 978-1-958263-14-3 hardcover
LCCN : 2023951541

MONSTERS IN LIFE AND LITERATURE

A Forensic Psychologist Reflects on the Nature of Good and Evil

PETER W. DEMUTH

Dancing Raven Press

THIS BOOK IS DEDICATED to all individuals who continue to humbly seek for truth, wisdom, and the embodiment of human wholeness, which includes both light and dark.

IN MY OWN SEARCH there have been four outstanding teachers who have provided me with direction in my professional growth as a person.

TO MY FATHER PETER JOHN, who taught me the importance of a good work ethic, how to persevere, and the importance of being dependable

TO DR. LLOYD STEWART, who believed in my abilities as a student and provided mentorship

TO DR. JAMES OLSSON, the person who invited me into the forensic psychological sacristy, and

TO DR. ALCIDES PINTO, boss, second father, friend, and overall mensch.

CONTENTS

PART ONE: VIOLENCE

PART TWO:
THE PSYCHOLOGICAL MAKEUP
OF MONSTERS

Foreword

AMONG THE BRUTAL HEAT and scorching hot sand, a human skull was found in Nataruk, Kenya. The skull had signs of a violent death caused by blunt force trauma. A trauma that was catalyzed by the hands of another human being. Brutal behavior among nomadic peoples, before settled human societies have arisen, provide indications that violence has been part of the human experience for as long as humans have existed. Although this particular story remains untold as the evidence has long been buried in the sand and the voice of the victim has long dissipated into the air, we can only speculate about the dynamics of how this situation unfolded which resulted in a level of violence that escalated into murderous death. Yet this violent encounter is not unique to the human experience. Fast forward to modern times. When we now think of vivid characterizations of violence, our minds often lead us to think of a psychopath. Psychopaths embody our most vivid representation of violent and callous behavior.

Dr. Peter Demuth, in his book, *Monsters in Life and Literature,* allows the reader to explore the inner workings of violent minds and takes you on a psychological journey to better understand the continuum of psychopathy. In order that the reader truly enters the hidden world of the psychopath, he weaves the concept of psychopathy with the biographies of fictional characters we are familiar with—those of the literary monsters found within the pages of famous books. Dr. Peter Demuth has encountered individuals on the spectrum of psychopathy in his extensive experience as a forensic psychologist. His broad range of clinical experience across multiple settings has culminated into a specialized world-view on the topic of psychopathy. Indeed, some of his work at a maximum security prison, a sexually violent offender clinic, and an inpatient psychiatric forensic unit, has provided him with ample opportunities to intimately encounter those with chronic mental illness, substance abuse issues, personality disorders and those who demonstrate psychopathic tendencies. As the Chief Forensic Psychologist in a state hospital he was a leader in the field overseeing the multiple forensic units that housed individuals who were unfit to stand trial, found legally insane and were too chronically mentally ill to be deemed as having the impulse control and behavioral norms to have the capability to live safely in society.

Dr. Demuth has taken his 30-plus years of experience working with psychopathy and combined those experiences with his expert knowledge of risk assessments, psychological evaluations, psychological disorders, and the criminal mind. He has combined these areas of expertise and applied his skillset to help us understand how psychopathy emerges, blossoms, and destroys, by applying his insight to fictional characters with whom we are familiar. Through lore, myth, and literary creations, the literary monsters you will meet on the pages of this book symbolize the good and evil in all of us. From psychopaths and criminals to fanatics and psychotics, these literary monsters embody our internal fears and hidden tendencies.

As Dr. Demuth illustrates, these human conditions do not exist in a fixed stationary spot on the dimension of human violence. In addition to being a clinical forensic psychologist, Dr. Demuth is also a Jungian Analyst and thus approaches this fascinating topic through the lens of Jungian theory. As Carl Jung stated, we all have a "shadow" and we all possess a hidden dark side. Dr. Demuth illustrates how an individual can develop an adaptive tendency to either adhere to social values and norms or conversely, an antisocial tendency that leads them to function more within the dark adaptation spectrum of the continuum. This concept is expertly depicted in this book as you will read where Dracula, Frankenstein, and the Werewolf, among the other literary monsters, exist on the continuum, albeit at different locations. By reading the psychological journey of these literary monsters, we get absorbed by their struggles and conflicts because they mirror our own internal selves. Fictional characters always reflect some aspect, conflict or anthropomorphic quality in us. This is why we love to get wrapped up in a good book or get absorbed by a good movie. We recognize aspects of our own self played out on the pages of a book or on the images of a screen. We will cheer for the heroes when we recognize the familiar themes of hope, longing, and love being played out. We will also be fascinated with the villains as the darker themes of revenge, jealousy and annihilistic rage may speak to our hidden fears and suppressed aspects of our personalities. Whatever the hero or villain pulls in us will be familiar, as it is part of our collective experience and consciousness.

In reading the vivid depictions of monsters in this book and assessing where they would fall on the dark adaptation process, Dr. Demuth discerns the various dimensions that would culminate in a monster becoming darkly adaptive. He not only explains the psychological process of dark adaptation, he also utilizes an existing measure of psychopathy to assess the level of psychopathy each literary monster has. This applies real-life behavioral science to fictional personages which is an extraordinary merging of the realms between reality and fantasy.

In reading this book, I was captivated by Dr. Demuth's innovative process of appraising literary monsters on the scale of psychopathy. Like Dr. Demuth, I too am a clinical forensic psychologist, who recognizes the dark aspects of psychopathy through the characters that Dr. Demuth writes about. I have spent 25 years working in the field of forensic psychology, assessing those who have committed violent crimes ranging from murderers, sexually violent predators, arsonists, gang members to career criminals who habitually burglarize and sell drugs. My assessments have taken me to jails, probation offices, outpatient and inpatient psychiatric units, private practice offices, and a command center mobile unit when I work as part of a hostage negotiations team. Working in these settings, with a broad range of individuals who are criminally minded, results in the development of a forensic intelligence whereby you learn to ascertain the overt and nuanced signs of psychopathy for your own self-preservation. When you work in a jail, you quickly learn to recognize the distinctly jarring sound of heavy steel doors as they slam behind you. You also learn to quickly decipher the facial and behavioral cues of the inmate to rapidly determine if he or she will be cooperative, irritable, or dangerous. This survival instinct becomes more developed over time as your exposure to these situations expands.

Learning how to quickly discern where on the dark adaptation process the person in front of you lies is an incredible asset to have whether you work in the field of forensic psychology or you are going about your day to day life. And lest you think that you will not encounter psychopaths in your life, Dr. Demuth will illustrate how these dimensions of psychopathy exist in our everyday world. From the ruthless CEO to a crime that has been committed in your neighborhood, you will gain insight into the deep inner world of the psychopaths who walk among us. Not many individuals who read this book will have the direct and immersive experience of sitting across from a psychopath like Dr. Demuth or myself, however you may encounter them in the next book you read, the next movie you watch, or more unfortunately, in real life. Reading this book will grant you the insight that took over 30 years for Dr. Demuth to gain and expertly cultivate.

The archetype of the psychopathic mind has always existed. Indeed, if you scroll through the pages of time and decipher hieroglyphics, read the bible, or unearth long lost weapons at archeological sites, you can see that early written history has portrayed the various massacres, warfare, and individual violence enacted by one human being onto another. Notwithstanding, these same early forms of writing have also reflected themes of benevolence and empathy on the same continuum as the opposing traits of apathy and psychopathy. Dr. Demuth will give you a rare view into how these individuals have developed a dark adaptation using the framework of literary monsters with whom we are familiar and whose stories embody our inner struggles, and by virtue of these struggles, embody the duality of the good and evil that exist in all of us.

—Dr. Alexandra Tsang, Forensic Psychologist

Prelude

DURING MY DOCTORAL INTERNSHIP in clinical psychology at the Crownsville Hospital Center just outside Annapolis, Maryland, my internship director Dr. Pinto was gracious enough to let each of the interns, six in total, spend one day a week off campus to pursue our individual interests—as long as we got our assigned hospital duties completed. I had the distinct privilege of spending one day a week at the Superior Court of Baltimore under the supervision of James Olsson, Chief Clinical Forensic Psychologist.

I picked my off-site location with Dr. Olsson due to a long interest in the law, beginning in the early 1980s when I worked as a counselor with the Second Chance program in the Queens Burrough of New York City under the direction of Joel Carlson. That program was designed to take remorseful, first-time young offenders, with misdemeanor charges and provide them with a second chance to redeem themselves by having their charges absolved, along with an opportunity to receive on-the-job training in a good paying job.

Now, forward several years, with the addition of a masters and doctoral degree, Dr. Olsson was introducing me to the art of forensic evaluations. He helped me to hone my abilities to interview and to assess an individual's competency to stand trial, as well as their ability to distinguish right from wrong (criminal responsibility/*mens rea*). He provided me with wise guidance in developing the judgment to predict, with a reasonable degree of psychological certainty, a person's potential to display future criminal activities.

Research, truth be told, has often indicated that psychologists have not been very good at predicting the future, so humility was a personal trait that Dr. Olsson and I talked about for many hours. We discussed his evaluations of John Hinckley, the man who shot President Reagan, and other famous cases, including his recording of over 700 Rorschach responses from Arthur Bremer, the man who attempted to assassinate George Wallace during the Presidential primaries on May 15, 1972. While the Rorschach manual would have suggested stopping the test well before 700 responses, the case was so important that the then young Dr. Olsson was not taking any chances of coming up short with his data collection. He knew that the more data you have the better prepared you will be in providing the answers that will be most helpful to the Courts.

During my training I was given the opportunity to evaluate unique individuals accused of a wide range of offenses. Additionally, I was allowed access to both files and videotaped interviews of all the major cases that had been evaluated by the Baltimore Forensic Medical Office under the direction of Dr. Jonas Rappaport. These cases included murderers, rapists, sexual offenders, and cases of domestic violence.

I was also assigned to be the treating therapist for one of the most notorious graffiti artists in Baltimore, who had been referred to therapy as part of his court ordered rehabilitation.

HENRY

One individual who caught my attention was the case of Henry, a 21-year-old white male who had murdered several family members, including his paranoid schizophrenic mother, his grandmother, as well as an aunt and uncle. All these folks lived in the same house.

His story is a tragic, cautionary tale that will sound like many of the current violent news stories appearing nightly on our television sets. Here is a brief synopsis of his life and murderous activities. Henry was the youngest of two boys, both born out of wedlock. His older brother was nine years older than Henry, and this brother left home at age 17 to escape the less-than-ideal conditions in the home.

For starters, as mentioned above, Henry's mother was a paranoid schizophrenic who was frequently a patient in several psychiatric hospitals. Her ability to care for and nurture Henry were severely truncated. He was often left to fend for himself and people familiar with the household environment described the residents as secluded, withdrawn, and seclusive.

Henry was also born with several physical abnormalities including web fingers on his left hand. The record indicates that he encountered social and emotional abuse throughout his life. He recalled an incident at age eight where he was thrown down a hill by his brother and some of his brother's friends, resulting in a laceration to his head. He hurried home to ask for his mother's help to stop the bleeding. His mother responded by acting indifferent – and telling him, "That's what you get when you eat catsup."

Henry, it was reported, would spend days just rocking back and forth in a rocking chair, crooning to himself. He was harshly disciplined by an uncle and oftentimes had soap rubbed into his eyes. He disliked school, was ostracized by his classmates, and felt that he failed in everything that he attempted to do. He had no close friends except for an alcoholic neighbor, a friendship he bought by giving this man money to obtain alcohol.

At age nine Henry was mandated to a Children's Home for three years, due to problems of neglect in his home. During this time, he frequently eloped from this facility and always returned home—only to be sent back. At age twelve he went to live with his first foster family. The foster mother noticed, after a week, that Henry was hiding his left hand in his pocket. She had not been informed about the deformity, and Henry was trying to hide it from her. The compassionate woman arranged for Henry to have plastic surgery, but this didn't change his behavior. He still hid his left hand in the pocket of his pant leg. This placement lasted less than a year after the woman caught Henry attempting to strangle her cat.

Henry was then transferred to another foster placement where he was surprisingly able to remain for about four years. However, he never made any friends and would sometimes throw stones at passing children to the dismay of the parents in the neighborhood. He would also catch frogs and turtles and play with them for a few hours and then torture them to death by beating them with stones. It was noted that he was also enuretic and that he once set the woods on fire behind his house.

Henry stopped attending school in the ninth grade. Interestingly he had no juvenile police record and had never used drugs or alcohol. Neither was he ever hospitalized for psychiatric reasons. He never worked and never had a girlfriend. His typical day consisted of reading books, smoking cigarettes, and writing secretly about killing people. He would destroy these writings every now and then due to his fear that they would be discovered.

He stated to the psychiatrist during his evaluation after his arrest that, "If they found my writings, they would know what I was up to, and what I was planning. Then they would have done something to stop me. Something would have been done and then nothing I was planning to do could have happened." He stated that the writing helped to steady him. It gave him something to do and gave him purpose.

A fine line, it seems, remained between his being steadied in a fantasy world and his acting out that fantasy in the real world. He would listen faithfully to the radio searching for guidance and signs about what to do. Henry believed that one station was God's voice giving messages within the program and that one station included encoded messages from Satan.

This was, in essence, an example of Henry's inability to work through and manage his disparate thoughts and feelings. He lacked the help of a healthy functioning ego that could tolerate this particular "tension of opposites" and work to integrate them.

Henry became enamored with the music group Queen and was especially fond of the song 'Another one bites the dust.' Henry seemed apparently happy and enlivened by these lyrics and by the thought that someone else was subjected to suffering, a similar pleasure he obtained by torturing frogs and turtles.

Somehow, by torturing these living creatures he felt less alone in his suffering. This dynamic represents a tragic example of the cliché, "'Misery loves company.'" At some point Henry won a sizable amount of money from the State Lottery, and this allowed him to purchase several guns that would be used in his offenses.

During the video interview with the psychiatrist Henry

displayed no remorse or empathy toward his victims. He seemed to enjoy recalling the killings, and he smiled when providing the chilling details. After locking his addled mother in the kitchen, he coaxed his uncle out of his bedroom by stating that a sink was overflowing. He then shot this uncle from behind in the head. He then shot his aunt, who appeared in the hallway after hearing gun fire. When he entered the room where his grandmother resided, she implored him not to shoot, stating "Oh Henry, please don't do that." Despite her pleas he shot her dead. Finally, he returned to the kitchen and pointed the gun at his mother. She apparently was cognizant of what was happening, but only in a partial way. Henry then shot her pointblank in the face.

When asked if he thought about killing anyone that day, during the interview, Henry stated no. When the psychiatrist asked him how anyone could be sure that he was no longer a danger to anyone, Henry responded with a smile, stating, "There's no way to be sure." Henry was diagnosed, like his mother, with paranoid schizophrenia. He was found NGRI, Not Guilty by Reason of Insanity and committed to a psychiatric facility.

BIGGEST LESSON LEARNED

As I now reflect, the biggest lesson from this period was that people don't always tell the truth. While training to be a psychologist, I thought that people were coming to me for help and that they would naturally tell, in full measure, what was going on. In normal cases it is usually only half the truth. In forensic cases it is seldom the truth. So, a certain naïveté had to be put to rest in me, while another inchoate skill, namely the ability to see reality as it really is, and not as I wished it to be, was being born out of a prolonged labor. I yearned to understand, why human beings commit crimes. I wanted to explore what happens to a person's conscience—that voice inside the head that says: "Don't do that. It's wrong." I was very aware of that voice in my own head. The Catholic nuns at Saint Agnes Elementary School, along with my parents, had taught and drilled it into me. I thought, didn't everyone have such a voice? Yet even with such questions, I had to admit that I didn't always follow that voice in my own head. It is just not a linear, automatic process 100% of the time. Otherwise, humans would be more like robots.

After my year-long internship I continued to work in the forensic field. I was hired at a maximum-security prison where treatment, as contrasted with punishment, was emphasized. The focus on treatment was unusual as far as prisons go.

There were only two correctional institutions in the whole United States at that time, to my knowledge, that put treatment first—the place where I was going to work, Patuxent Institution in Maryland, and Atascadero Prison in California.

People are usually locked up to pay a debt to society. You commit a crime, and you do your time. Politicians and wardens may say that rehabilitation is a focus in their prisons, but in my experience, this has usually been just window dressing.

Patuxent Institution, however, was a different entity. In addition to the Warden and correctional staff, we also had a Medical Director and a Director of Clinical Services, and three fully staffed clinical teams—comprised of psychologists, social workers, and psychiatrists—who evaluated and treated the inmates who were accepted into the program. And yes, an offender had to be first screened and then deemed appropriate beforehand to avail him or herself of such a valuable opportunity.

In addition to my work as a team psychologist, I was asked to develop and direct a drug treatment program at the prison, due to my background in addictions, acquired while in a master's program at Loyola University, as well as my work at the National Institute on Drug Abuse's Addiction Research Center in Baltimore, Maryland, recruiting drug research volunteers from the streets of Baltimore and serving as the Center's psychometrician. Insider humor had it that the Patuxent Drug Recovery Program, or PDRP, was really named for my initials rather than for "Patuxent Drug." So yes, a serious job can still include room for humor and light-heartedness.

Across the street from Patuxent Institution were our two sister institutions, the Clifton T. Perkins Hospital for the criminally insane, and the Maryland Penitentiary, otherwise known by its nickname 'the Cut.' It got that sobriquet because its campus was cut in two by an active railroad line. In addition to the nearby local Howard County jail, there was one other large facility in the area, approximately 17 miles east by northeast, namely the Baltimore Penitentiary, where the State's gas chamber was kept in good repair though unused for many years.

During my post internship years, I also served as a group therapist at the University of Maryland's Violent Sexual Offenders Clinic in Baltimore, again under the direction of Dr. Olsson. During this period, it became increasingly clear to me that all individuals do not operate with the same level of intellect, emotional control, forethought, knowledge, and concern for consequences. I came to feel empathy for some of my patients. The idea that some individuals function from a 'diminished capacity,' is a concept that is usually deemed unworthy by those dedicated to the 'letter of the law.' Diminished capacity suggests that by dint of some mental defect or disease an individual is incapable of making a plan that would qualify as "guilty intent." That being the case, it seemed ludicrous to judge everyone by a single standard, that is, by the letter of the law, which is rigid and allows for very little discretion. I was looking for and aspiring to add 'the spirit of the law' into my considerations. The concept of extenuating circumstances is a similar concept that comes into play during the sentencing phase. This acts to reduce the severity of the sentence after consideration of the individual's background factors such as upbringing, family supports, past trauma, and addictions. This part of the legal process helps to balance punishment with human compassion.

After four years at the Patuxent Institute, I returned to the Crownsville Hospital Center where I had interned to serve as the senior forensic psychologist. Two years later I was promoted to Assistant Chief of Psychology and began learning the art of running a Psychology Department under the tutelage of Dr. Alcides Pinto, whom everyone fondly referred to as "El Hefe"— the Chief. I truly admired, respected, and loved Dr. Pinto and would sign future letters to him, outlining my subsequent adventures, post Crownsville, with the familiar 'su hijo', "Your son." Dr. Pinto, you see, had several lovely daughters but no sons. Since we had a close collegial and personal relationship, he affectionately referred to me as the son that he wished he had had. I had lost my father several years earlier and took this as a touching gift. Unfortunately, Dr. Pinto succumbed to the Covid 19 virus in 2021.

In 1998, my wife and I relocated to Chicago. She had been offered a great opportunity to work in affordable housing. I was hired at the Elgin Mental Health Center (EMHC) as both the Assistant Chief Psychologist and as the Director of Clinical

Training. EMHC was, at that time, the largest forensic hospital in Illinois with over three hundred beds, divided evenly between court ordered cases involving competency to stand trial and assessment of criminal responsibility and those with civil commitment involving threat to self or others or inability to care for self.

In 1999 I was promoted to Chief Forensic Psychologist while retaining my oversight of the training of Psychology externs and interns. In addition to my usual forensic focus, I also gained additional expertise in the assessment of dangerousness and took the lead responsibility in determining when to give patients increased levels of privilege, based upon their ability to demonstrate increased awareness and emotional control.

In this process of risk assessment, I developed an ability to discern the steps and elements that coalesced into each patient's problematic behavior. It became clear to me that when you stabilize any one ingredient in the chain of events that has resulted in problematic behavior, contributing factors such as job loss, relationship conflicts, drug or alcohol abuse, the failure to take prescribed medication, and the state of homelessness, the potential for a repeat negative outcome can be significantly reduced.

This information remains essential in constructing the relapse prevention plan. It is an indispensable tool for all involved—the criminal offender, the released psychiatric patient, and the monitoring professional or treatment team that will be responsible for supervising the individual during their probation, parole, or post discharge stabilization period.

I remember being in a staff meeting when we were evaluating the potential release of a patient who had sexually molested several children. The team psychiatrist stated that he thought it was time to release the individual because he had not abused any children in the three years that he had been in the hospital. In fact, he had been a model patient and demonstrated no untoward behaviors on the unit. That was the psychiatrist's reasoning for recommending the patient's release. I felt strongly that that was very shortsighted on his part. I asked the treatment team how many children this patient had encountered since his admission. The answer was zero. That was the same amount of confidence that I placed in the psychiatrist's opinion. The patient was not released, and the treatment team revisited and revised the steps necessary to enact a more thorough treatment plan to ensure patient growth and the public's safety. Again, this underscores the importance of everyone being grounded in reality. Not all clinicians are.

In 2005 I left the Elgin Mental Health Center to build my private practice and to pursue another area of interest, Analytical Psychology. I applied to and was accepted for analytic training at the C.G. Jung Institute of Chicago. I completed my training as a psychoanalyst in 2012 and continue to have enthusiasm for my work. I view every day as a new opportunity to grow. The reflections in this book blend my 33-plus years of forensic experience with my appreciation for the work of C.G. Jung.

THE CONCEPT OF EVIL

It is my opinion that the word 'Evil' is an overused, emotionally laden term. It is often used, conveniently, to describe the behavior and intentions of individuals who commit acts that may or may not be criminal but certainly do not cross the threshold for being Evil—at least in the way that I will define the term. Evil, in my view, must always involve an act that is intentionally and morally wrong. It is something bad by design. It is wicked on purpose.

Criminal acts, while they can be horrific, seldom meet this level of intentionality. Therefore, we must not be too quick to pass judgment on an individual's character without first studying, and more importantly, attempting to understand the underlying causes and factors that result in the individual's behavior.

Equally important, is the understanding of our own thoughts and behaviors which we can easily project onto others for a variety of reasons, mostly defensive, thus clouding any clarity that might be achieved.

SOCIETY AND SUBJECTIVE VERSUS OBJECTIVE TRUTH

Society, in its wisdom and ignorance, will always require that its members adhere to basic laws and values. Acting for the greater good of all is a basic tenet for a civilization to first coalesce into an organized structure and then to flourish.

The question of what represents the greater good, however, can often pit an individual intra-psychically against themselves or another individual, one group against another group, and lawyer against lawyer. This greater good, which we aspire to achieve, upon deeper inspection, is largely subjective. It may not adhere to the objective facts of a situation, choosing instead a path subjugated to a particular goal—one that does not necessarily advocate the collective good. It is society's challenge to provide the framework or structure from which the larger truth can be made manifest and supported.

In the following pages, I will discuss the subjective view-points of multiple characters and work to develop an objective understanding of their perspectives. In this effort I will embrace the spirit embedded in the words of the Roman philosopher Terrance (190-159 BC), when he stated: "Homo sum; humani nil a me alienum puto." [I am man, I count nothing human foreign to me.]

All the characters studied in this book will fall predominately into one of the following categories: Monsters, Fanatics, Psychotics, Psychopaths, Criminals, or individuals with underdeveloped or stunted ego strength. Conspicuously missing from this list are the categories of mental illness and personality disorders. The reason for these omissions is that the above stated categories will all encompass some aspect of mental illness or a personality trait, which can then be discussed and delineated within each type as appropriate.

Certainly, the categories of psychosis and the underdeveloped ego will encompass issues related to mental illness, and the psychopath will display the most pernicious aspects of personality disorders. Each of these general categories, however, is not meant to be exclusive as there will inevitably be overlapping traits and behaviors that manifest across descriptions. This allows for some diagnostic flexibility.

Monsters represent phantoms born of internal fears and archetypal components of the psyche. They are internally constructed by an individual's unique experiences and social surround.

Fanatics are individuals who see things through the narrow lens of uncritical enthusiasm, zeal, and passion. They are wholly committed to their objective and believe that their actions are justified. They do not seek to include all the possible facts or possibilities, however, in their calculations, only those that reinforce their own position.

Psychotics have problems with their reality testing. They can see things, smell things, hear things and imagine things that are real to them but not real to others.

Psychopaths lack empathy, display shallow affect, prey upon others, lack a sense of remorse, and enjoy a sense of their own imagined superiority. Criminals are a heterogeneous group of individuals who commit acts deemed injurious to the public welfare, and for a multitude of reasons.

Finally, there are those individuals who lack ego strength and are prone to bouts of either anxiety or depression. In such states judgment is compromised and diminished to the point of being overly compliant, dependent on an authority, or prone to inflation.

Of all the above designations, only the psychopath passes this writer's litmus test for Evil 99% of time. I reserve the 1% to allow room for debate, and for the theoretical possibility of redemption. All categories, nonetheless, will fall along a continuum comprised to a greater or lesser degree of both good and bad, or an interplay between light and dark forces.

In the end, it will be up to each of us, singularly or collectively, to decide just how much each attribute is present in any given case. The larger, and more important question in deciding where an individual falls on this continuum, might just be: How capable is an individual in exercising self-determination? Furthermore, how much is the behavior in question under the influence of unconscious factors. Such unconscious factors, that is, if you believe that there is such a thing as the unconscious, can flood and overpower a person's ego and deprive it of sane, rational judgment.

I will touch upon these issues and wrestle along with the

reader to find answers to these questions. That said, the headlines that scream "The accused killed his wife in a state of rage" should alert us to question just how much control an ego has at such a juncture, as it is the ego, which represents an individual's center of consciousness and control, his or her seat of judgment. That is the part of the person that we will hold accountable.

PART ONE

Violence

CHAPTER 1

A BRIEF INTRODUCTION TO HUMAN VIOLENCE

The whole of life is nothing more than questions that have taken unto themselves shape, and bear within themselves the sum of their own answer: and answers that are pregnant with questions. Only fools see it otherwise.

—MEYRINK, 1976, 73

HUMANS HAVE ALWAYS POSSESSED a morbid fascination with violence, the antisocial person, and the associated acts committed by such individuals. Violent and Evil themes permeate our myths, our spiritual teachings, our literature, our entertainment, and our psychological theories. Violence and the struggle between acceptable and unacceptable behavior play a part, subtle or not so subtle, in our everyday relationships with ourselves, our intimates, and with the relative strangers around us. W.E.B. Du Bois pointed out that the stranger that causes us the most difficulty may turn out to be our own self:

Herein lies the tragedy of the age: not that men are poor, all men know something of poverty; not that men are wicked, who is good? Not that men are ignorant, what is truth? Nay, but that men know so little of men. (1905, 161)

Each of us faces this challenge of right versus wrong in his or her own unique way and with varying degrees of success. It is a fluid situation and requires constant adjustment and care. Thankfully, the majority of us manage to be generally law abiding, non-violent, and productive citizens, turning out to be decent human beings when measured by the yardstick of the law. For that we should all be thankful. That said, however, there are still many dangers to be both aware of—and prepared for.

WE VERSUS THEM

Generally, there is an omnipresent wish on the part of human beings to divide the bad, Evil doers into the 'them' category and to place the righteous, good ones into the 'we' category. Ironically, many of the identified 'bad ones' probably see themselves as primarily good.

This penchant to rid oneself of the bad and to see it in others is directly related to the Jungian concepts of projection and shadow. Projection is that tendency to put into others what we most wish to avoid in ourselves. According to Samuels, Shorter, and Plaut (2000) projection allows "difficult emotions and unacceptable parts of the personality to be in a person or object external to the subject. The problematic content is thereby controlled and the individual feels a (temporary) release and a sense of well-being." (113)

This thing that we wish to avoid in ourselves is our shadow. Our shadow interferes with the way our persona is currently and consciously constructed. The persona is an edifice that tries to represent us in a particular way to the outside world. It is not our authentic self, however. Jung stated that the shadow, in contrast, is the "thing a person has no wish to be." (1985, ¶470) It represents "… all the unpleasant qualities one wants to hide, the inferior, worthless and primitive side of man's nature, the other person in one, and one's own dark side." (Samuels et al, 2000, 138)

Baumeister (1997) stated, "Most people who perpetuate Evil do not see what they are doing as Evil. Evil exists primarily in the eye of the beholder, especially in the eye of the victim." (1) And if something doesn't affect us directly, we tend to simply ignore it or to not place it high on our priority list. This, of course, is a self-serving act of omission. Furthermore, most people view truly violent or hideous acts as falling somehow outside of the general repertoire of the everyday man and woman.

By constructing such a psychological barrier between ourselves and the individual who commits horrific acts, we gain a sense of security that reinforces our own sense of goodness. Under closer scrutiny the adage 'If not for the grace of God go you or I', seems indeed closer to the truth than most of us are willing to accept.

It is interesting, however, that individuals who have been convicted of crimes are much less likely to see themselves as separate from society. They readily see the potential bad in both themselves as well as in others. They readily want to include everyone in the category of the potential criminal, perhaps for the inverse reason that the so-called good people want to separate themselves out.

While working at the prison in the early 1990's, one of the frequent statements uttered by the inmates with whom I worked therapeutically was: "Everyone does something wrong, Doc. What have you done? Don't try to play innocent with us." I would often-times simply respond to the inmates by saying that whatever my behavior has been it hasn't landed me either in trouble with the law or sent me to prison. But still their questions hit home, and while I felt smug on one level, on another, I recognized that my response had been both defensive and inane. Had it been simply luck that had separated my life's course from those I was there to treat? I recalled many actions as a youth, that, if I had been caught, my life might very well have taken a different direction. I benefitted from several guard rails including involved parents.

This reminds me of a funny story told to me by a colleague, Dr. Don Carroll, about the film maker John Waters, known widely for the film *Pink Flamingoes*, who had previously taught a course to the inmates at this same prison on the art of film making and general theatrics. As the story goes, one day an inmate accosted Mr. Waters by asking him what crimes he had committed. Mr. Waters, with a straight dead panned face replied: "My films are my crimes." His response was much wittier and more genuine than my own.

Misunderstandings, regarding violence and antisocial individuals, however, are also perpetuated by a sensation-seeking media. Reporters oftentimes see a story as a way to attract viewers and to sell newspapers, magazines, and books. The phrase "Breaking news" is overused to the point of nausea. And the truth is a commodity that can be largely misrepresented or totally disregarded at times in the service of titillation, economics, and the quest for personal fame and success.

The world of publishing is a very competitive one, and it appears that truth is sometimes the least important part of what is being written or reported. On multiple occasions over the years, award-winning journalists have been fired by such newspapers as the Boston Globe and the New York Times for making up facts and fabricating individuals and events to create a sensational storyline. According to Baumeister:

> It has become clear to nearly everyone in journalism that the entertainment value of the news coverage is more effective in attracting an audience. One must tell the public what it is interested in hearing, and often this means presenting simplistic explanations that confirm the expectations, beliefs, and prejudices of the public. Some journalists do not see themselves in the business of educating the public so much as of informing it of what it is interested in hearing about. (1997, 81)

In response to the media's coverage of certain events, as well as humankind's acceptance of the superficial, conversations at the proverbial water cooler continue to be punctuated by such naïve questions as:

How could anybody do such a thing?

Is this individual from some other planet?

Is he or she or it a member of some spin-off mutant species who falls outside the pale of humanity?

Is such a person possessed by the devil or by some other kind of demon?

Is he or she the personification of pure Evil?

Such questions go on and on and could even be worthwhile if they resulted in additional focused research and further understanding. But it seems that human beings, when given the chance, do not want to dwell on unpleasant topics or memories if we can avoid them.

Most individuals want to be entertained instead of educated, noticed instead of noted. While humans have made enormous technological progress, I believe that we have not advanced emotionally and psychologically as a species and fail to make use of the knowledge that is available to us.

Without the effort to grow emotionally and intellectually en masse, humanity continues to be lulled into a state of non-awareness or participation mystique. Participation mystique is a term that Jung borrowed from the anthropologist Lévy-Bruhl (Samuels et al, 2000). It refers to a state in which a person becomes enmeshed with an object, another person, or a group and can no longer distinguish where he or she ends and the object begins.

Without the developed skill to differentiate self from other, our ability to be conscious is largely compromised. We, in essence, abdicate our responsibility to be fully awake. As the saying goes: "If ignorance is bliss, tis folly to be wise."

However, in regards growth, another saying by Santayana, "those who cannot remember the past are condemned to repeat it." (1905, ch.12) applies equally and parallels a quote often attributed to Einstein when defining insanity: Doing the same thing over and over and expecting different results. There is no evidence that Einstein actually said this, but that doesn't negate the fact that it embodies a good deal of wisdom, whoever said it.

Adaptation and the Continuum between Good and Evil

While Mona Lisas and Mad Hatters,
Sons of bankers, sons of lawyers,
turn around and say good morning to the night.
For unless they see the sky,
but they can't and that is why,
They know not if it's dark outside or light.

—John & Taupin, 1972

One does not become enlightened by imagining figures of light but by making the darkness conscious.

—C.G. Jung, CW 13, ¶335

All human beings have an inherent potential for both pro-social and antisocial behavior. Whether a person demonstrates a proclivity toward goodness and good citizenship, or badness and criminal behavior will be the result of multiple factors, some obvious and some not so obvious.

Influences such as genetics, social environment, attachment styles, mental illness, culture, fantasy, psychological development, drug and alcohol abuse, or a response to some life-defining experience, such as trauma, can set a person off in a particular direction to perpetuate something good or bad.

More commonly, an individual becomes a composite of both potentials and tends to lean one way or the other depending

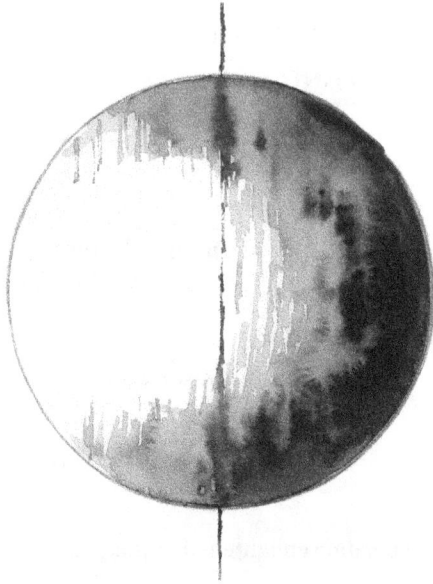

Diagram 1. The Continuum between Good and Evil

on the influences that affect them. As a result, they will fall at some point along a progressive/regressive continuum, which I refer to as "the continuum between Good and Evil," illustrated in Diagram 1.

At one extreme there is an absence of antisocial tendencies, suggesting an entirely pro-social/saint-like individual, whereas on the other extreme there is an overriding influence of severe psychopathy, represented by a totally antisocial/evil individual. These extreme poles symbolize, in essence, the undiluted states of Good and Evil, the places held by familiar archetypal figures, namely God and the Devil, respectively in our religious traditions.

Human beings, embody one of the extremes only when the individual's ego has been overwhelmed and the personality has been captured, seized, and possessed by an archetypal force emanating out of the collective unconscious. Such a predicament was faced by Dr. Jekyll in his encounter with Mr. Hyde, which we will address in Chapter 9.

In the middle of the continuum, consciousness, judgment, and good reality testing reside. Movement away from the middle deprives, by degree, an individual's ability to exercise what philosophers have called free will.

A movement toward either pole gradually takes an individual further into the realm of unconsciousness. Every individual, however, continues to possess, in potential, access to either side of this psychological good/bad continuum as is symbolized by the Chinese concept of Yin and Yang where there is always a dot of light in the dark and always a spot of dark in the light.

One can imagine the machinations of a tightrope walker as they cross a deep gorge. It takes great balance and relaxed concentration to execute the on-going corrections to not fall off the rope. It is my opinion, however, that even psychopaths have some potential to re-balance themselves, though let me be clear, this is unlikely.

Based on an individual's preferences and conditioning, an individual will tend to gravitate toward that place where he or she feels most emotionally at home. In some cases, a person will remain entrenched, and frozen there. Upon closer examination we will also see that everyone's point of balance may not be the center point upon which most of us agree.

Remember, it is not the actual event that creates reality. Instead, it is each person's interpretation of the event that creates his or her reality. What may puzzle many of us is the observation that many criminals and psychopaths appear to be quite sane.

When you ask if they would commit such an act if a 'policeman' was standing next to them they would be able, without effort, unless they are psychotic, to reply that they would not act if the policeman was watching. To act would put them in jeopardy and prevent them from completing their objective. This observation does not mean that 'good judgment' is at work. Other aspects of this individual's reasoning ability, sometimes unobvious or unde-tected at first glance, can be quite delusional. It simply means the individual cunningly prefers not to be caught. In this matter I have found Pinel's (1801) term for these individuals *manie sans délire* (insanity without delirium) to be most instructive. Just because someone appears sane doesn't mean that they are. James' comment regarding individuals who can adjust in life versus those who seem entrenched is quite enlightening:

> There are people for whom Evil means only maladjustment with things, a wrong correspondence of one's life with the environment. Such evil as this is curable, in principle at least, upon the natural plane, for merely by modifying either the self or the things, or both at once, the two terms may be made to fit, and all go merry as the marriage bell again. But there are others for whom evil is no mere relation of the subject to par-ticular outer things, but something more radical and general, a wrongness or vice in his essential nature, which no alter-cation of the environment, or any superficial rearrangement of the inner self, can cure, and which requires a supernatural remedy. (1902, 114-115)

But what is this supernatural remedy that James talked about? And how can it be made available to the individual in need?

Is it the state of Grace? Is it a visit from the Holy Spirit? Is it an experience of unconditional love? Whatever it is, it seems that it is beyond the sole direction or intention of the ego. Jung commented:

> We are still so uneducated that we actually need laws from without, and a taskmaster or Father above, to show us what is good and the right thing to do. And because we are still such barbarians, any trust in the laws of human nature seems to us a dangerous and unethical naturalism. Why is this? Because under the barbarian's thin veneer of culture the wild beast lurks in readiness, amply justifying his fear. But the beast is not tamed by locking it up in a cage. There is no morality without freedom. When the barbarian lets loose the beast within him, that is not freedom but bondage. Barbarianism must first be vanquished before freedom can be won. This happens, in principle, when the basic root and driving force of morality are felt by the individual as constituents of his own nature and not as external restrictions. How else is man to attain this realization but through the conflict of opposites? (1990, 213)

Jung also stated:

> Insight into them must be converted into an ethical obligation. Not to do so is to fall prey to the power principle, and this produces dangerous effects which are destructive not only to others but even to the knower. The images of the unconscious place a great responsibility upon a man. Failure to understand them, or a shirking of ethical responsibility,

deprives him of his wholeness and imposes a painful frag-
mentariness on his life. *(Memories, Dreams, Reflections, 193)*

DARK ADAPTATION

To introduce my concept of Dark Adaptation, I would like to begin
with Plato's Allegory of the Cave. It concerns a short conversation
between Socrates and Glaucon about the attainment of pure truth
and how one's physical or subjective environment can enhance
or shackle this quest.

Here is the beginning of their discussion (1-3):

> **SOCRATES:** And now let me show you in a figure how
> far our nature is enlightened or unenlightened: Behold!
> Human beings living in an underground den, which has
> a mouth open towards the light and reaching all along
> the den; here they have been from their childhood, and
> have their legs and necks chained so that they cannot
> move, and can only see before them, being prevented by
> the chains from turning round their heads. Above and
> behind them a fire is blazing at a distance, and between
> the fire and the prisoners there is a raised way; and you
> will see it, if you look, a low wall built along the way,
> like the screen which marionette players have in front
> of them, over which they show the puppets.

> **GLAUCON:** I see.

> **SOCRATES:** And do you see men passing along the wall
> carrying all sorts of vessels, and statues and figures of

animals made of wood and stone and various materials, which appear over the wall? Some of them are talking, others silent.

GLAUCON: You have shown me a strange image, and they are strange prisoners.

SOCRATES: Like ourselves, and they see only their own shadows, or the shadows of one another, which the fire throws on the opposite wall of the cave?

GLAUCON: True, how could they see anything but the shadows if they were never allowed to move their heads?

SOCRATES: And the objects which are being carried in like manner they would only see the shadows?

GLAUCON: Yes.

SOCRATES: And if they were able to converse with one another, would they not suppose that they were naming what was actually before them?

GLAUCON: Very true.

SOCRATES: And suppose further that the prison had an echo which came from the other side, would they not be sure to fancy when one of the passersby spoke that the voice which they heard came from the passing shadow?

GLAUCON: No question.

SOCRATES: To them the truth would be literally nothing but shadows of the images.

GLAUCON: That is certain.

SOCRATES: And now look again, and see what will naturally follow it, the prisoners are released and disabused of their error. At first, when any of them is liberated and compelled suddenly to stand up and turn his neck round and walk and look towards the light, he will suffer sharp pains; the glare will distress him, and he will be unable to see realities of which his former state he had seen the shadows; and then conceive someone saying to him, that what he saw before was an illusion, but that now, when he is approaching nearer to being and his eye is turned towards more real existence, he has clearer vision, what will he reply? And you may further imagine that his instructor is pointing to the objects as they pass and requiring him to name them,—will he not be perplexed? Will he not fancy that the shadows which he formerly saw are truer than the objects which are now shown to him?

GLAUCON: Far truer.

SOCRATES: And if he is compelled to look straight at the light, will he not have a pain in his eyes which will make him turn away to take in the objects of vision

---

which he can see, and which he will conceive to be in reality clearer than the things which are now being shown to him?

GLAUCON: True.

The inspiration for my Dark Adaptation heuristic did not initially come from Plato. It came from my studies in physiology and my review of the occipital lobe and vision. I became fascinated by the idea that a dark-adapted eye represented a progressive ocular condition brought about through exposure to complete darkness over a considerable period, not unlike the folks in Plato's Allegory of the Cave.

This adaptation was also characterized by a progressive increase in retinal sensitivity to light (Van De Graaf and Stuart, 1988). The reader may recall from basic physiology, that the cones are the cells in the retina sensitive to light and color, whereas the rods are the cells in the eye that do not register color and can adapt to darkness, which we experience as absent of color.

Each type of cell has its designed purpose depending on the visual conditions present. Most individuals have a capacity to adjust back and forth between the light and the dark, but it is reasonable to assume that the longer one stays in any one condition the ability to adjust back to the other, or even the desire to adjust back, becomes compromised and truncated.

In other words, an individual can feel discomfort in the presence of light and will prefer the dark or stay in the shadows whenever possible. Simply put, we are to a large degree, conditioned by our environment. Our perceived sense of knowledge comes from our phenomenological experiences. Might character and one's worldview simply be a matter of adaptation to what we have become accustomed to?

I have borrowed and generalized the term Dark Adaptation, based on the adapted eye model, as an analogous way to explore the process by which an individual can become antisocial or criminal in his or her orientation, either because of genetics, through exposure to a particular social environment or culture, internal psychodynamics, or some life-defining moment, such as physical, emotional, or sexual abuse, or a combination thereof.

Over time, an individual can develop a pronounced adaptive tendency to either adhere to pro-social values or to lean in a more antisocial, or self-centered direction. Wholeness of personality, however, requires an ability to access both.

Throughout this book I will make use of a variety of Jungian concepts to amplify important etiological issues. I will also highlight a number of established forensic concepts such as diminished capacity, impulse control, Johnson's (1949) term superego lacunae, brain damage, Lonnie Athens' five stage model of violence, and Freud's Id, Ego, and Super Ego triumvirate, among others, in order to demonstrate how motivational concepts such as guilt, conscience (the inner voice of guidance), free will, and self-discipline (ego-based) can all fall short if relied upon to corral and contain the potential antisocial tendencies in all of us. I will also introduce the concept of Psychological Allergies, an idea akin to Jung's complex, as an additional heuristic to assist in deepening our understanding.

In each chapter in the second part of this book, I will make use of one of several familiar literary figures, namely *Dracula*, *Frankenstein*, *The Phantom of the Opera*, *The Werewolf*, *Dr. Jekyll and Mr. Hyde*, *The Pied Piper*, *The Golem*, and Wilde's *Dorian*

Gray to put "flesh and bones" onto manifestations of the Dark Adaptation process. I will then place each character at the point along the continuum that corresponds to his or her level of good, evil, and psychopathy by rating them with the use of the Hare Psychopathy Checklist-Revised, a psychometric tool that I will discuss in further detail in Chapter 2.

CHAPTER 2

PINPOINTING THE LEVEL OF VIOLENCE AND PSYCHOPATHY IN AN INDIVIDUAL

TO UNDERSTAND HOW AN individual operates the assessor needs to pinpoint where he or she falls on the Dark Adaptation Continuum. To accomplish this, one can employ a few well-researched assessment instruments. Three of the most helpful and informative choices from my experience have been:

- The Hare Psychopathy Checklist-Revised (Hare, 1991),
- The Psychopathic Personality Inventory (PPI-R) developed by Scott Lilienfeld and Brian Andrews (2005), and
- The Lonnie Athens' Model of Violentization (1992).

All methods place a heavy premium on the individual's background and history. The Psychopathy Checklist—Revised (PCL-R), with which I am most familiar, focuses on the individual's overall level of Psychopathy. The PPI-R looks closely at several conceptual constructs, some of which overlap with the PCL-R, while the Athens' approach maps out the individual's exposure and movement through four distinct developmental stages that, if completed, qualifies the individual as a bona fide dangerous, violent criminal.

THE HARE PSYCHOPATHY CHECKLIST-REVISED (PCL-R)

The Psychopathy Checklist—Revised (PCL-R) is an assessment instrument based upon the extensive research of Robert Hare and his colleagues in Canada. It was built upon the earlier work of Cleckley (1941, 1976) who identified many of the original personality traits that correlate highly with the concept of Psychopathy, a condition that would place someone at the far-left end of the Dark Adaptation Continuum.

Psychopathy, it is important to note, has been shown to be highly correlated with violence and criminal behavior. Hare stated, "In addition to their high rate of criminal activities in general, psychopaths engage in an inordinate amount of violent and aggressive behaviors ." (1991, 55) Furthermore, Hare and McPherson found that, "... psychopaths defined by the PCL were significantly more likely than other criminals to engage in physical violence and other forms of aggressive behavior including verbal abuse, threats, and intimidation." (1991, 55)

Psychopaths are self-centered, egotistical individuals who are indifferent, unable, and/or uninterested in forming close empathic relationships with others. They lack an emotional connection and view others solely as objects to be manipulated for their own needs and gratification. This failure to experience empathy largely separates those who can be treated therapeutically (the antisocial) from those who cannot (the psychopath). Without empathy, there is no resonating authentic and genuine link between human beings. Empathy allows us to 'feel into,' not just 'think into,' another person's experience and to recognize them as a person in his or her own right. Successful treatment, in either a mental health system or a prison, geared at reintegrating a person back into society, requires such a connection and an ability for intra-psychic integration.

Psychopaths live among us, but not with us. They act according to their own set of rules. Developmentally they are very much like the uncivilized two-year-old child who has not yet learned the meaning of the word 'no.' The two-year-old, however, is responsive emotionally to the reactions of important adults to his behavior and can begin to internalize social and moral rules.

The psychopath, on the other hand, may have a biologically based deficit to respond appropriately to the emotional reactions of others to his behavior. Meloy stated: "Psychopathy is a deviant developmental disturbance characterized by an inordinate amount of instinctual aggression and the absence of an object relational capacity to bond." (1988, 5) The capacity to bond is what helps attenuate aggression: the capacity for empathy causes inner discord when experiencing the effect of aggression on someone the child loves.

In Table 1 (next page) is a list of the twenty characteristics that comprise the PCL-R. These characteristics have been intensely researched and shown to be significantly related to the concept of psychopathy. A single symptom is not pathognomonic of the condition by itself. Ergo, the more pieces of the puzzle that you have in your makeup, the clearer the gestalt.

Psychopaths, interestingly, make up about 25% of the prison population (Meloy & Gacono, 2000). In terms of overall numbers, research suggests that about 1% of the general population may meet the diagnostic requirements of the psychopath (Hare, 1993, 2). This

TABLE 1
THE PSYCHOPATHY CHECKLIST—REVISED

1. Glibness / Superficial Charm
2. Grandiose Sense of Self Worth
3. Need for stimulation / Proneness to Boredom
4. Pathological Lying
5. Conning / Manipulative
6. Lack of Remorse or Guilt
7. Shallow Affect
8. Callous / Lack of Empathy
9. Parasitic Lifestyle
10. Poor Behavioral Controls
11. Promiscuous Sexual Behavior
12. Early Behavioral Problems
13. Lack of Realistic, Long-term Goals
14. Impulsivity
15. Irresponsibility
16. Failure to Accept Responsibility for Own Actions
17. Many Short-term Marital Relationships
18. Juvenile Delinquency
19. Revocation of Conditional Release
20. Criminal Versatility

suggests that one person in 100 is psychopathic, while one inmate out of four is psychopathic.

Evaluators are cautioned, however, to take great care in their decision-making process before labeling an individual a bona fide psychopath, because such a label can have far reaching consequences (Hare, 1985a).

It is my personal experience and opinion that the "true" psychopath is rarer than these numbers suggest. I would place the percentages, based on my use of the PCL-R, at the prison where I worked, at between 10 and 15% of the prison population.

The diagnosis of Antisocial Personality Disorder, which is mistakenly interchanged with the concept of Psychopathy by the public, is a much more prevalent diagnosis in the prison population and is a condition which is more amenable to treatment efforts.

Each of the PCL-R's traits is rated on a three-point scale where a score of 0 = absent for the trait, 1 = maybe or partial, and 2 = definite regarding how much the particular trait exits within the individual being evaluated. A range of scores has been established to measure the presence and extent of psychopathic traits. The score on the Psychopathy Checklist is used by professionals to categorize individuals according to their level of intractability when making decisions about (1) the potential benefits of treatment, (2) the achieved level of rehabilitation resulting from treatment, and (3) issues affecting public safety.

When I was directing the PDRP, the evaluation for admission first addressed this question: Was the person's drug use the result of a criminal lifestyle or was the criminal lifestyle the result of drug addiction? It was theorized that individuals who were addicted to drugs and became criminal to support their habits were more treatable contrasted to individuals who were involved in criminal activities before they became addicted.

Next, we considered the PCL-R score. Generally, a score of 30 was used as a cutoff score for the diagnosis of Psychopathy. Scores between 25 and 30 also received a lot of attention, especially when additional information, if provided, could raise the overall score.

Hare cautions professionals who use the Psychopathy Checklist-Revised to make sure that they have received the prerequisite training in the utilization of this instrument to ensure its proper use and scoring. This advice, of course, should be followed regarding the use of any psychological assessment measure (American Psychological Association Ethical Principles, 1992, 1.04 b) to assure the reliability of the assessment results. This writer has received the requisite training through several workshops and has administered well over 300 PCL-Rs.

Let me now briefly provide the reader with an example of how I would use the PCL-R with a client based on an actual case with some information altered to protect the confidentiality of the individual involved.

MR. A

Mr. A (Anonymous) was an educated, physically fit, fifty some-thing white married male, father of four, working at a financial institution. He reported imbibing in three or four glasses of wine during the week but denied the use of any illicit drugs. He was charged with multiple counts of child molestation including fondling, inappropriate touching, and fellatio. He had no previous arrests or convictions, and was a heretofore respected person in the community.

During my evaluation of Mr. A, he expressed shame and remorse over his criminal actions and stated that he felt inclined, despite his resolve to never again engage in such criminal behaviors, to warn others about himself because "they have the right to protect their children." This expression of remorse and his public confession was apparently admirable, though probably self-serving to some degree as his case had not yet been adjudicated. Concomitantly, his intention to get treatment and to never again abuse another child was a first step toward rehabilitation – though, as usual, it too came only after he has been accused and convicted of his offense.

It would have been preferable that he would have come forth on his own and turned himself in to the authorities, but that is usually not the way it happens. That said, determining the genuineness and depth of Mr. A's commitment was difficult to ascertain. That's why the court wanted and needed to have some basis on which to base their decisions about sentencing and length of sentence, and so they turn to folks such as myself for guidance.

Mr. A disclosed a history of erectile dysfunction (ED) for at least 20 years. He had never sought medical treatment. The ED apparently surfaced shortly after Mr. A was laid off from his job, and he was subsequently out of work for a time. He found himself under increasing bouts of stress and experienced decreasing self-confidence.

The ED interfered with his intimacy with his wife, and this in turn led to an increasing sense of isolation and distance from her, someone who had been a mainstay in his overall life balance.

He began to find relief in masturbation and made frequent visits to adult bookstores, where he could view pornographic movies in a private booth. He also began to actively fantasize about a young girl lying on a bed and exposing her breast.

When Mr. A was out walking, he would often get a thrill if he would see a young girl sitting in such a way that she was not "very careful about how she positioned her legs." These voyeuristic behaviors initially remained in shadow, but they slowly began to take up a greater portion of his time in behavior, daydreams, and thought processes.

While they remained largely kept in check, for a period, by his heretofore normal lifestyle as a good citizen who attended church and other functions with his family, these shadowy behaviors began to gain a reinforcing potency and larger influence over him. Indulging in fantasy it seems required no need on Mr. A's part to perform under the spotlight. Fantasy produced no fear of failure, and his performance anxiety was greatly reduced because he controlled the fantasy and its contents.

This inadvertently served as a slippery slope allowing Mr. A to inch toward acting out his fantasies with an actual victim. This victim turned out to be a young neighborhood girl of twelve in whom he sensed vulnerability.

He told me that "I saw her as kind of an underdog and wanted to somehow help her to feel better about herself."

This was his way to rationalize his otherwise abhorrent behavior and further loosen the tethers of reality. He saw it as a way that he could help her while all the time the actual purpose was to selfishly help himself to manage his growing desperation, a desperation produced in the psyche where the ego is both partially aware and unaware that it is on a collision course.

Mr. A reported that once he had acted on his fantasy, and he succeeded, 'everything else seemed to take a back seat and was secondary to this new thrill." He admitted to feeling some anxiety at times, prior to his arrest, but did not recall feeling anxious while engaging in his devious and illegal behavior with a minor. Test and interview results suggested the following diagnoses for Mr. A (*Diagnostic and Statistical Manual, American Psychiatric Association - V [DSM-V]*, Axis I):

Pedophilia, Non-exclusive type. 302.2
Dysthymia, late onset. 300.4

Mr. A. scored a total of 10 on the Hare Psychopathy Checklist (PCL-R), which suggests non-criminal, non-psychopath. (See Mr. A's results on the next page.)

Mr. A. was not a psychopath. He also didn't meet the criteria for Antisocial Personality Disorder. He would not be a good candidate for prison either as he would be threatened, abused, and likely in harm's way for the duration of his time there. But he did need to pay a debt to society. Based on the sentencing guidelines and the recommendations of experts that I consulted in this area, I recommended 18 months in a local jail. The idea was to require him to pay his societal debt, be remanded to on-going treatment with qualified professionals, during and after his time behind bars, and then to restore him to society, where he still had a loving and supporting family, despite what he had done. These cases are not easy, and it is hard to keep a balance between the desire for punishment, disgust at the behaviors involved, and the desire to be fair to all the parties involved.

HARE PSYCHOPATHY CHECKLIST (PCL-R)

Results for Mr. A

TRAIT	SCORE
Glibness / Superficial Guilt	0
Grandiosity	0
Need for Stimulation	2
Pathological lying.	0
Conning / Manipulative	2
Lack of Guilt / Remorse	1
Shallow Affect	0
Lack of Empathy	0
Parasitic Lifestyle	0
Poor Behavioral Controls	1
Promiscuous Sex Behavior	1
Early Behavioral Problems	0
Lack of Realistic Goals	0
Impulsivity	1
Irresponsibility	1
Failure to Accept Responsibility	1
Many Short-term marriages	0
Juvenile Delinquency	0
Revocation of Conditional Release	0
Criminal Versatility	0

TOTAL 10

THE PSYCHOPATHY PERSONALITY INVENTORY-REVISED

The Psychopathy Personality Inventory (PPI-R), first developed by Scott Lilienfeld and then later revised as the Psychopathy Personality Inventory-Revised (2005) with input from Michelle Windows, attempted to build upon the earlier work of folks like Cleckley and Hare.

Its purpose was multifold including an attempt to 1) further clarify the boundaries of psychopathy with other seemingly over-lapping disorders such as Antisocial Personality Disorder; 2) to provide a fuller identification of what psychopathy consists of both at a global functioning level as well as its various component parts, and 3) with developing a tool that could be administered by a trained, non-psychologist, technician, in a relatively short amount of time, and be applicable to populations beyond the correctional setting such as mental health clinics and community health centers. The PPI-R consists of the following 8 content scales:

1. Machiavellian Egocentricity (ME)
2. Rebellious Nonconformity (RN)
3. Blame Externalization (BE)
4. Carefree Nonplanfulness (CN)
5. Social Influence (SOI)
6. Fearlessness (F)
7. Stress Immunity (STI)
8. Cold-heartedness (C)

The PPI-R also includes a self-report section, constructed at the 4th grade reading level, that collects a 'self-reflected' piece of data from the individual being assessed. All in all, this instrument provides another tool and angle to assess and identify psychopathy in individuals.

THE LONNIE ATHENS' MODEL OF VIOLENCE

When people look at a dangerous, violent criminal at the beginning of his developmental process rather that at the very end of it, they will see, perhaps unexpectedly, that the dangerous violent criminal began as a relatively benign human being for whom they would probably have more sympathy than antipathy (Lonnie Athens, 1992, 6).

The Athens' model of violence offers the reader another road map into the development of an individual's violent behavior. What may be most important about the Athens' model, however, is that it offers some hope, both for future generations of potentially violent individuals and their potential victims, as well as those who have not yet completed the sequential steps that are required in the creation of a dangerous violent criminal.

Athens believes that with appropriate early intervention, the violent actions of many of these individuals may either be reduced or prevented altogether especially if there are counter balancing positive influences from significant others.

To become a dangerous violent criminal according to Dr. Athens, an individual must pass through and complete four distinct stages including:

- ⊚ Brutalization
- ⊚ Belligerency
- ⊚ Violent Performances, and
- ⊚ Virulency.

STAGE ONE: Brutalization

Brutalization is comprised of the following three sub-stages:

- Violent Subjugation
- Personal Horrification
- Violent Coaching

Violent Subjugation occurs when a significant strong authority figure, such as a father, uses violence to force the individual to do his or her bidding. Violent subjugation can be practiced in two distinct ways, namely with coercion or with retaliation.

With coercion, the use of threat or actual violence to get the other person to submit is geared at beating down the other person's resistance by violent force or intimidation. Once enough fear is generated, the fearful person will usually give into the other's demands to avoid additional anxiety, fear, or actual bodily harm.

Thus, a sense of dominance gets established between the aggressor and the victim. An example is the character Theon, a prince from the Iron Islands, in the *Game of Thrones, Season 2*, who was broken down into submission by the tyrannical Ramsey.

After each capitulation, there is usually some initial relief on the part of the victim as the threat of or the actual physical attacks abate due to his or her compliance with the aggressor. The individual gains an understanding as to how to placate the attacker and how to prevent further suffering at their hands.

There's an old saying that when you're getting hit in the head with a hammer, it sure feels good when you stop getting hit in the head with the hammer. Ironically, the opposite can also be true. A person can take great pride in being able to withstand pain and to take whatever the other can dish out.

My colleague Gus Cwik once reminded me about the character Will in the film *Good Will Hunting* (1997). In this film Will, who has been physically abused by his father, says "I would rather get hit with a pipe than with a belt—because fuck him—fuck the aggressor!" His ability to take the harsher of the two punishments represents a form of psychological strength. Such strength is what helps Will to survive the continuous beatings from his father and to develop the persona of the 'tough guy' as he moves into the outside world. This stance, however, while adaptive to the family, will cause much difficulty in the outer world beyond the family.

Shortly into the brutalization process there occurs a mounting sense of humiliation on the part of the victim. The submitting person begins to feel as though their sense of self has been taken away unjustly, which it has. There is, as a result, a mounting desire for revenge. Revenge, however, is oftentimes only experienced in the victim's fantasy world because the subjugator is bigger and more powerful and would likely, if this internal revenge were detected, by the aggressor, snuff it out by squashing it with great force.

So, without an actual route to revenge, fantasy can serve as a temporary container to keep hope alive internally by helping the victim to retain some sense of self-respect and a way to manage shame until the day comes when the victim can get even. When the victim capitulates and submits to the will of the subjugator the technique of coercion has been successful. No other threat or use of force is then required.

Personal Horrification

If the technique of coercion is not sufficient for the aggressor to keep the subjugated person in check, the violent person may decide to up the ante using retaliation. The aggressor can meet a perceived resistance on the part of the victim with a force many times greater than what is needed to put down such resistance. It is not enough to have the person merely submit to the aggressor's will: the victim must be taught some type of lesson and punished for his or her disobedience or display of disrespect. This reinforces the aggressor's sense of omnipotence.

Athens contends that an individual does not have to be the actual victim to begin the process of becoming a dangerous violent criminal. It is sufficient to witness such violence, as in the case of a son witnessing the constant physical and emotional abuse of his mother.

The child may be horrified at what is happening and have the urge to go to his mother's defense. But alongside the thought of going to his mother's assistance is the realistic likelihood that he too will be demolished if he attempts to intervene. What can a little boy do against such ferocity and primitive muscle except to fantasize about future retaliation when he grows stronger with age?

The key point to keep in mind here is that a person feels dominated and controlled and threatened and there is virtually nothing he or she can do about it. Athens calls this experience "personal horrification." In the case of the son witnessing his mother's beating, a burning rage can begin to slowly simmer and develop. This rage replaces the original feelings of helplessness and provides the victim with a means to both imagine and to plot the sweet fruits of revenge. This represents the first step toward becoming a dangerous violent criminal.

I recall an incident several years ago when I accidentally veered my car into another person's lane. The guy that I unintentionally cut off came roaring up beside me in his truck, yelling obscenities and giving me the finger. I yelled something back along the lines of "grow up" and thought that was the end of it. It was not. At the next light the guy ran into the back of my car and pushed my car into the vehicle in front of me.

Before I knew what was happening, a shadow passed on my left and then a hand flew through my open window punching me in the face. I was stunned. I got out of the car with my nose bleeding and stood my ground while he went on yelling and gesticulating. While part of me wanted to punch him back, I simply waited for the police to arrive.

The guy continued to yell as though he was the real victim. The police finally arrived and took down the report. This guy told the police that I had hit him first. There was no doubt in my mind that that was how he felt. At the court hearing the judge ordered him to pay for my broken glasses and for my lawyer's fee. This settlement did not seem sufficient considering all the time and effort that went into seeking justice.

That said, I believe that this story illustrates two important points. First, this guy felt as though I had disrespected him and that he had to correct the score. He was not going to let me get away with such a major slight. The second point I wish to make is that I felt like a 'wimp' for not having punched the guy back. Something in my upbringing spoke to me about standing up and not allowing a bully to take advantage. So, even though I did the right thing and followed the law (waited calmly for the police), part of me had been desirous of 'pumping my chest' and of settling the score in a more primitive manner. Failure to do so resulted in an experience of my own, though to a much lesser degree, of personal horrification, which lingered on for some time. A part of me, albeit a small part, felt ashamed of myself for cowering under such intimidation.

In a more recent event, I was driving into a parking lot, and a man walked across my path. He had just come out of the brewery that was to my right and was apparently inebriated. As it looked like he was intending to walk in front of my car, I slowed down. He began yelling at me. I stopped my car and rolled down my window to inquire what was wrong. He yelled that I was going too fast. When I attempted to reason with him, he shouted: "Get out of here, you asshole!"

I rolled the window up and slowly drove away. But for the rest of that day and for a few days later, I felt infected by a certain negative contagion. I was not able to relax and just let it go. When you deal with such an individual, they can project a certain noxious element into you that disturbs your soul. It can give you a direct experience about what they are dealing with and why they would want to project it away from themselves and onto you.

Violent Coaching

The final component of Stage One in the Athens' model involves the concept of 'violent coaching.' During this phase the victim is taught how to deal with people who cross or disrespect him.

The student of the subjugator is taught never to pacify or ignore any challenge or insult. It does not matter whether the insult is minor, imaginary, or real. In all cases there is only one appropriate response and that is that the transgressor needs to be taught a lesson.

During the process of 'violent coaching' the heretofore victim gradually becomes a victimizer. This process has oftentimes been referred to as an *identification with the aggressor* (White &

Gilliland, 1975, 105). In Case 2 in Athens' book, *The Creation of Violent Dangerous Criminals* (1992), one victim described a few of the finer points that were imparted to him by his father during the coaching process:

> My father told me that there were two things I better always remember. If you ever get into it with anybody, don't ever run but stand there and fight. If something is worth fighting about then it's worth killing somebody over. If you get into a fight with anybody, try to kill them. I don't care who it is—a man or woman—pick up a stick, board, rock, brick, or anything, and hit them in the head with it. That way you won't have to worry about having any trouble from them later. (50)

The coaching serves two major purposes. First, it supplies the victim with a route or mechanism to attenuate his or her own fears and anxieties through narcissistic inflation and concomitant bravado. Second, it provides the individual, who may continue to suffer at the hands of his or her coach, the techniques to eventually fight back.

STAGE TWO: Belligerency

The experience of Stage One leaves the individual with lingering pangs of inferiority, as well as a desire to escape from a sense of humiliation and self-deprecation. While the lessons of violent coaching have provided some sense of relief in the form of self-protecting aggressive techniques, at least in the victim's fantasies, the individual has usually not yet had an opportunity to test them out.

In Stage Two, the individual discovers that by taking the initial steps toward violent action against others who, in their own mind have provoked them, they too can begin to sense the potential power that has, up to this point, vicariously been observed in their coach.

The apt pupil begins to first rationalize and then to whole-heartedly believe that "resorting to violence is sometimes necessary in this world" (Athens, 60). He or she begins to test out this growing discernment and discovers that it can work to perfection. He or she carefully starts out, slowly at first, to display belligerence (verbal aggression), and studies the reactions of others.

When he or she senses fear, there is recognition that this fear is the result of his or her behavior. There is a subsequent psychological inflation—a felt sense of power. It can feel quite intoxicating. He or she then becomes a budding master of pushing other peoples' buttons.

In turn, the fear that is created in others increases the bully's own inflated (narcissistic) sense of self. At this point, however, most of the individual's behavior has only been an inching toward actual violence. Aggressive posturing, hostility, apparent threats, and the proverbial beating of one's chest, all serve to put others on notice.

When there is an unexpected strong resistance on the part of the potential victim, however, the aggressor may back down at any point and re-evaluate the situation more thoroughly. This possibility to re-evaluate is slowly drained of its potential once the individual moves deeper and deeper into the process of "Violentization."

Up to this point, there has not been a full-fledged call to violence. *Most importantly, this stage not only serves as the launching pad toward actual aggression, but it also represents another opportunity for some type of alternate direction to take hold.* For example, if sufficient positive elements can be introduced into the person's sphere the potential toward violence can be attenuated. Influences from a mentor, a teacher, an uncle, a big brother, a parish priest, a lover, a successful acceptance on to a sports team, a prolonged visit to another locale, or any genuinely positive experience in life, can tilt the person's orientation back toward more pro-social possibilities. Such influences can keep the individual from working his or her way further along the Dark Adaptive Continuum in the wrong direction. Each degree further along the continuum and away from the middle, represents another hurdle to overcome if ever a return trip is attempted.

I once had a patient who was physically and emotionally abused by his father. He was traumatized, especially by the unpredictability of his father's abuse, and this interfered with his subsequent ability to form close relationships with others. Yet he grew up to be a kindergarten teacher who felt deep empathy for each child's development. He wondered how this was possible that he could care so much about children and concluded that he never wanted to be hated like he hated his father. He would refuse to let this destructive force loose into the world. He would contain it and make sure that it died with him, which might be another, better way, to take revenge against the toxic influence of his father.

STAGE THREE: Violent Performances

During the third stage in the Athens' model the individual begins to test out his or her violent inclinations. He or she has observed how the techniques have worked firsthand during Stage One.

The individual has also fantasized on multiple occasions about seeking revenge against the original subjugator.

The individual has also learned during the Second Stage how to "jerk people around" and to "get their goat," using belligerency and verbal posturing. Now comes the time when the individual seeks to put into practice all that he or she has learned—to put all the pieces together into a whole action.

There is still the uncertainty of Stage Two about whether they have what it takes and whether fantasized power will work. Will they, for example, be able to threaten and scare and dominate another person as they have fantasized to themselves? Everything it seems, points to the probable success of violence.

All that remains is an actual successful experience with violence to make it real. Once he or she succeeds with violence, the confidence to aggress against others has a poured foundation that will quickly solidify and be ready to be further build upon.

STAGE FOUR: Virulency
Stemming from the graduated "successes" that the individual has experienced in Stage One, Two, and Three, he or she now begins to experience a growing sense of *virulency*. The old insecurities and self-doubts are quickly being sealed over, dissociated from by a sense of indestructibility. There is an ever-widening desire to educate the world and all its residents that 'no one messes with me.'

As mentioned before, this can become a godlike state that does not allow for any dissent. Historical persons such as Stalin, Hitler, Saddam Hussein, Idi Amin, and Putin, our most recent example, come directly into mind when envisioning the embodiment of godlike virulency. Athens cautions the reader to take note that "nothing expands a person's determination to be violent more than the repeated successful performance of violent action" (1992, 71). Athens also reminds us "it must not be forgotten that while fame may be morally superior to infamy, their impact may be remarkably similar. (96)

CHAPTER 3

FACTORS THAT INFLUENCE VIOLENT BEHAVIOR

Psychological Allergies, Complexes, Archetypes, Constitutional Traits, Behavior Repertoire, the Fallacy of Free Will, and Good versus Evil Intent

Society prepares the crime. The criminal commits it.

—CHINESE PROVERB

MANY FACTORS INFLUENCE A person's ability to make good decisions in life. A good decision can be loosely defined as a person's ability to choose something that benefits him or herself without harming others. Jung when defining the concept of individuation, insisted that the process of individuation always served both the person and society. (1973) It also included a capacity to put someone else first if his or her need is judged to be the greater one. The importance of a solid psychological foundation, otherwise known as a mature ego, cannot be overemphasized.

Built upon a nurturing and supportive environment, especially in early developing childhood years, a healthy ego creates a bulwark against future threats and is the best preventive medicine.

But what happens when these essential ingredients are not present in sufficient quantities? What happens when a person's psychological base is inadequately prepared to handle what the world will dish out?

While we may all be born equal in the ideal sense of the word, we do not all grow up with equal intellectual and emotional abilities. Each of us is not afforded the same level of talent, support, or opportunities in life. All potentials, oddly enough, begin with the premise that we do. Like the beginning of the baseball season, every fan imagines that their team will be able to compete with the Yankees.

Perhaps that is also why parents and teachers often fail to detect the early warning signs that are almost always present. A parent wants to believe that their child will be able to compete and succeed. But right from the start there are inequities.

Some of these inequities can occur within a certain environment or culture and may be accepted as just the way things have always been. Like water, most individuals tend to follow the path of least resistance. We are more instinctive than consciously intentional. Individuals may only notice or admit to a problem when it slaps them in the face.

Jung made the following comment that is very germane to this discussion: "We know that the mask of the unconscious is not rigid. It reflects the face we turn towards it. Hostility lends it a threatening aspect, friendliness softens its features. (CW12, ¶29)

And so, the relationship between consciousness and the unconsciousness can be a partnership or a cold war. Most of us, given the chance, will avoid or turn away from unfriendly faces, but this doesn't necessarily dissolve the problem at hand.

Does it then follow that the criminal, the monster, and even the saint, who may emanate from the same initial place—eventually veer off into a distinct place created by the relationship between the conscious and the unconscious and the individual's environment?

The criminal/monster has a "dark" and unfriendly orientation with the unconscious while the saint/non-criminal has a more "light" and friendly relationship. Unfriendly and friendly tend to lead to different outcomes though both are rigid in their orientation. Each inelastic construction will attempt to limit the potential of the other side, and this works against the potential for wholeness.

There are countless folks who have paid attention to these psychological stances. Freud for one, noticed "among adult criminals we must no doubt expect those who commit crimes without any sense of guilt, who have either developed no moral inhibitions or who, in their conflict with society, consider themselves justified in their actions." (1916, 333)

In his study of delinquent behavior, Aichorn (1925) identified factors that cause an individual to reject societal values. He looked especially at the influences of *extreme indulgence and overvaluation* (a tendency toward narcissism) on the one hand, and *excessive harshness and depredation* on the other. This dyad of indulgence/overvaluation and excessive harshness/depredation represents a "tension of the opposites" that pulls an individual toward an extreme, something that I will discuss in detail in later sections of this book.

Following up on Aichorn's observations, Abraham observed

that certain conditions in the background of individuals who demonstrated antisocial tendencies tended to give them a nudge toward a criminal lifestyle. Abraham stated:

> We often come across the results of early pampering, which intensifies the child's demands for love to the extent which can never be adequately satisfied (narcissistic). Among delinquents (antisocial) we are more likely to come across a different fate of the libido in early childhood. It is the absence of love, comparable to psychological undernourishment, which provides the precondition for the establishment of dissocial traits. An excess of hatred and fury is generated which, first directed against a small circle of persons, is later directed against society. (1927, 304)

Franz Alexander (1930) also tried to tease out differences underlying criminal behavior. He proposed four levels of pathology that reflect a hierarchy of the ego's ability to restrain itself from unconscious impulses. These four levels in order of greatest to least capacity are: neurosis, neurotic character, psychosis, and true criminality.

Alexander believed that 'neurotic character' was the essential building block of psychopaths. He further believed that neurotic characters act out their conflicts because they have a diminished capacity to transform these conflicts intra-psychically into something more acceptable and beneficial to the community via Freud's ability to sublimate. Alexander stated:

> They live out their impulses, many of their tendencies are asocial and foreign to the ego, and yet they cannot be

considered true criminals. It is precisely because one part of such an individual continues to sit in judgment upon the other... that his total personality is easily differentiated from the more homogeneous, unified, and antisocial personality of the criminal. The singular and only apparently irrational drive to self-destruction met with in such people indicates rather definitely the existence of inner self-condemnation.

Their conduct arises from unconscious motives which are not directly accessible to their conscious personality... Admonition, encouragement or punishment coming from the environment is as useless as his own resolution, "I am beginning a new life tomorrow.

A large proportion of such individuals, neurotically driven by unconscious motives, now to commit a transgression, then to seek punishment, sooner or later fall afoul of the law.

Their lives are full of dramatic action...something is always happening, as if they were literally driven by the demonic compulsion... Here is where the adventurers belong whose manifold activities give expression to an underlying revolt against public authority. They always manage to be punished unjustifiably from their highly subjective point of view (1930, 11-15)

Building upon Alexander's work, Karpman (1941) differentiated between two types of psychopaths, namely, the idiopathic individual who experiences no guilt whatsoever and the symptomatic individual who experiences guilt but at a more unconscious level. This latter type is close to what Alexander previously characterized as the neurotic character. This model provides additional support for efforts to assess an individual's level of psychopathy prior to providing treatment. Without guilt or the ability to empathize with another individual the whole basis for the therapeutic relationship and the soundness of its container is challenged. Without the ability, both intra—and inter-psychically, to relate to the other, there is no potential for individual transformation.

Otto Kernberg also took a keen interest in personality. While he was largely known for his research into borderline conditions, he also analyzed the dynamics involved with antisocial personality. He conceived psychological development as a hierarchical process and believed that individuals who have Antisocial Personality Disorder should be assessed and categorized from least to most severe. Kernberg stated:

> I have found that all patients with antisocial personality structure present severe narcissistic pathology, destruction of their internal world of object relations, and extreme and usually untreatable superego pathology. Such patients are at the limits not only of analyzability but also of treatment with any modified psychoanalytic psychotherapies. The evaluation of the quality of object relations, of superego pathology, and of the nature of pathological narcissism tells us whether the patient is treatable. (1984, 276)

John Bowlby (1973) also contributed much to our understanding of early infant development and its subsequent effect on adult behavior. During his research with children who had been separated from their 'care providers' he began to observe certain behaviors. For example, upon separation from the mother he noted that some children began to look about and to seek out for them. Other children, however, seemed to be unaffected by the mother's absence. He proposed three general styles of attachment—secure, avoidant, and ambivalent—which has provided us with a measure of an individual's ability to form close relationships with others.

According to Wallin "Secure babies appear to have equal access to their impulses when they feel safe and to seek solace in connection when they do not." (2007, 19) He continues, "Secure infants, however distressed by separation, were almost immediately reassured by reconnecting with their mother and readily resumed play." In contrast, avoidant babies continued to act independently and to explore their environment—showing no outward signs of stress or anxiety upon separation, although their cortisol levels, when measured, were extremely high. These children seemed unaware of the physiological fact that they were afraid and anxious. Finally, ambivalently attached infants tended to come in two varieties, angry and/or passive.

According to Wallin (2007), both types are preoccupied with their mother's whereabouts and, as a result, they are unable to freely explore their environments with a healthy curiosity. Upon the return of the mother ambivalently attached infants were slow to be reassured, and it took an inordinate amount of time for negative emotions to dissipate.

PSYCHOLOGICAL ALLERGIES AND COMPLEXES

One influence that can undermine a person's general quality of life is the presence of allergies. *Webster's New World Dictionary of the American Language* (1982) defines an allergy as "a hypersensitivity to a specific substance (such as food, pollen, dust, etc.)

or condition (heat or cold) which in similar amounts is harmless to most people." (36) Symptoms are described as irritating, bothersome, inundating, troublesome, and time consuming. They can also be restrictive as in the case of having to avoid certain foods or not being able visit a friend who has a pet. This represents a bother at best, excruciating duress at its worse, but uninvited in all cases.

Most of us, who are without a particular allergy, fail to appreciate the agony that some people experience. Those who have suffered from such maladies, however, usually demonstrate a higher degree of empathy.

Stemming from our knowledge of physiological allergies, the question arises as to whether there might be an equivalent condition in the psychological realm? Is it possible that things outside of our conscious recognition such as Psychological Allergies (a metaphor for Jung's complex) affect us much like physiological ones and cause some of us to have a hypersensitivity, albeit not to things such as dust and smoke, but instead to situations, emotions, individuals, groups of people, and experiences, especially those that involved pain, joy, or other strong emotions?

John Giannini (2010, personal communication), a colleague, believed that "all criminal behavior is an allergy." In all these scenarios there is an influx of archetypal energy that fills the person up where they have been empty or deficient. Let me now say a few words about archetypes, the foundation and primal source of all behavior.

ARCHETYPES

Jung's concept of the archetype, or a priori categories of potential functioning, helps to explain how things outside of one's immediate consciousness can and do influence our behavior. Jung stated:

It was this frequent reversion to archaic forms of association found in schizophrenia that first gave me the idea of an unconscious not consisting only of originally conscious contents that have got lost but having a deeper layer of the same universal character as the mythological motifs, which typify human fantasy in general. These motifs are not invented so much as discovered; they are typical forms that appear spontaneously all over the world, independently of tradition, in myths, fairy tales, fantasies, dreams, visions, and delusional systems of the insane. On closer investigation they prove to be typical attitudes, modes of action—thought processes and impulses, which must be regarded as constituting the instinctive behavior typical of the human species. The term I choose for this, namely, "archetype," therefore coincides with the biological concept of the 'pattern of behavior.' In no sense is it a question of inherited ideas, but of inherited, instinctual impulses and forms that can be observed in all living Creatures." (CW3, ¶565)

Archetypes are thus an important contribution to the present discussion on violence because they represent influences outside of a person's awareness. Archetypal energy can rush in to fill a void, especially during times of psychological anxiety and panic. They provide life with meaning and structure, or confusion and disarray. These archetypal energies represent, in essence, theoretical prototypes that have been built into our human psyches through repetition and the evolutionary process over the centuries. They are essential to human development and represent a potential to be tapped when certain repetitive human motifs are constellated. The maturity of the individual will ultimately decide to what extent the archetype will be used consciously and constructively. Conversely, the less mature and the less conscious an individual, the more likely that he or she will be used by the archetype. In this case, the archetype can have a compulsive quality to it.

Major archetypes include the father, the mother, the king, the devil, the leader, the wise old man, and the warrior. In the light of the recent plethora of terrorist attacks around the world a variation of the warrior archetype, namely the 'terrorist' (or holy warrior) seems to be emerging.

UNDER THE INFLUENCE

What is it like to be under the influence of an archetype? The narrator in the following soliloquy describes his predicament after he has been overpowered by something 'stronger' than himself. We might ask whether anyone can be held accountable in the strictest sense of the word for their lack of control during an archetypal possession? Let us now hear the narration of this individual in the throes of being possessed:

> When I committed my crime—and, please, I will ask you to spare me the relation of the details—it was so hideous, I think the mere remembrance of it would kill me to live through it again. But I had no choice in the matter. I had to commit it, though I was fully conscious at the time of what I did. Something inside me of which I had no previous knowledge,

came to life, and was stronger than I was. Do you suppose I'd have committed a murder like that, if it had been left to me to choose? I, who had never taken life—not even that of the smallest insect... and wouldn't be able to... even now. (Meyrink, 1976, 167)

CONSTITUTIONAL TRAITS

Everyone has encountered an individual who becomes angry at the drop of a hat, seemingly for the most innocuous of reasons. We characterize such individuals as having a 'short fuse' and of not being able to control his or her temper. But how often do we also wonder: Did he or she select this as an ideal behavior option? If able to, and accompanied by the reward of self-esteem, wouldn't this same individual choose to act differently if given a list of positive options and outcomes to choose from? Would such an individual consciously choose to act in an antisocial manner if given a legitimate choice to behave differently? Furthermore, what would happen if such a person were taught new behaviors? This is what we attempt to do when we provide therapy or 'rehabilitate' the people residing in our prisons.

But hold on a minute! Doesn't there always remain an underlying proclivity, certainly in the short run, to fall back on previously old, established behavior, especially behavior that has served some important purpose? For those of us who have worked in the prison system, it is certainly not earth-shattering news to find out that a parolee has become a repeat offender. Psychologists refer to such phenomena as a 'regression toward the mean,' an instance of 'spontaneous regression,' or as a failure of newly acquired pro-social behaviors to generalize to a new setting. The old behavior, in essence, lies in wait for the opportunity to reassert itself. It is, after all, not entirely eradicated from the psyche.

When the conditions become favorable the behavior can reappear almost automatically unless the person is vigilant and has a strategic plan to prevent this from happening. We call this a relapse prevention plan. We are Creatures of habit, and habits are hard to eradicate completely. Fortunately, as we replace old habits with new behavior, old habits can eventually lose their power over time, but only if the old behaviors are not further reinforced. To use behavioral terms, the process of non-reinforcement is called extinction.

The only problem here is that even with one slip up, such behaviors, even those that have remained dormant for many years, can resurface with renewed vigor, especially if the behavior which has replaced it is not exciting and not reinforcing enough. Interestingly, a colleague of mine at the prison used to remind us that the term rehabilitate might be a misnomer. He felt that some individuals had never been habilitated so how could we rehabilitate them? Inmates would also question some of our therapeutic techniques such as teaching them to talk about their feelings and to learn to control their emotions. They would challenge these notions by saying that when one is in the hood there isn't time to talk about feelings. If you snooze you can be dead! So, what we teach in therapy doesn't always generalize to the streets.

JUNG'S THEORY OF COMPLEXES
Jung's theory of complexes is similar to my idea of Psychological Allergies. Jung believed that:

Today we can take it as moderately certain that complexes are in fact "splinter psyches." The etiology of their origin is frequently a so-called trauma, an emotional shock or some such thing, that splits off a bit of the psyche. Certainly, one of the commonest causes is a moral conflict, which ultimately derives from the apparent impossibility of affirming the whole of one's nature. This impossibility presupposes a direct split, no matter whether the conscious mind is aware of it or not. As a rule, there is a marked unconsciousness of any complexes, and this naturally guarantees them all the more freedom of action. In such cases their powers of assimilation become especially pronounced, since unconsciousness helps the complex to assimilate even the ego, the result being a momentary and unconscious alteration of personality known as identification with the complex. In the Middle Ages it went by another name: it was called possession. (CW8, ¶204)

Like the often slow, insidious onslaught of the addictive process, a person under the control of a complex may think that they are in control —but after a certain threshold has been crossed, sound judgment and control become compromised. Then, once adapted to a certain psychological place, a person becomes comfortable in that place. And if one is comfortable in the dark, he or she can be classified as dark-adapted.

Emily Early, in reviewing the story of Stevenson's *Dr. Jekyll and Mr. Hyde*, referred to such an adapted state as a "**shadow-contaminated complex**." (1983, 31) I believe that this label can be very helpful. Early described the Dark Adaptation process very accurately when she stated that "... if we see Jekyll as symbolizing the ego, and Hyde as symbolic of the autonomous complex, we see Hyde taking more and more conscious energy, and we note that Hyde is acquiring will. (32)

Jung stated, "A complex begins with an affective [emotional] event." (CW3, ¶140). An affective moment involves either pleasure or pain. That is why the psyche pays attention to it and marks it as an important experience, which is stored unconsciously and also consciously. As noted by Samuels, Shorter, and Plaut:

> A complex is a collection of images and ideas, clustered round a core derived from one or more archetypes and character-ized by a common emotional tone. When they come into play (become constellated) complexes contribute to behavior and are marked by affect whether a person is conscious of them or not. They are particularly useful in the analysis of neurotic symptoms. (2000, 34)

Like the archetypes, complexes are bipolar by nature and can manifest as either negative or positive. (Hopcke, 1999,19)

CAIN: THE FIRST CRIMINAL AND THE POWER OF THE COMPLEX

To discuss the influential impact of constitutional traits in a person's life, I will now look at the Biblical character Cain. He was the first born son of Adam and Eve. It will be a constructive exercise to investigate what produced his criminal, murderous behavior. Was it caused by the environment, genetics, or some combination thereof? Can we even characterize Cain as a criminal based on his behavior or his lifestyle prior to the murder of his brother Abel using DSM-V criteria? Probably not.

The story of Cain and Abel is centrally about relationships. Relationships require the reciprocal ability to care for another person and to receive that other's caring in return. But in Cain's family all was not perfect. We know from the story in Genesis that Adam and Eve had their own set of difficulties beginning with the eating of the apple. Adam and Eve, you may recall, had been warned that, "From every tree of the garden you may surely eat. But from the tree of knowledge, Good and Evil, you shall not eat, for on that day that you eat of it, you are doomed to die." (Alter, 14)

This dynamic is like the story of Bluebeard's wife who was told that she could explore the entire castle in Bluebeard's absence except for one room. Such a temptation invariably is too hard to resist. And so, Eve is tempted by the serpent and she, in turn, tempts Adam to take a bite. When Adam is confronted by God over his actions Adam replies: "The woman who you gave to me, she gave me from the tree, and I ate." (Alter, 16) Adam thereby puts the blame on Eve, and she in her turn blames the serpent for beguiling her.

This is the beginning basis for the general albeit largely defunct idea (one can only hope) that the female of our species is the 'temptress' that will bring mankind down if she is left to wield her influence freely.

What's more important here is that there is no admission of responsibility on the part of either Adam or Eve. Their failure to accept responsibility is characteristic of many individuals. Not taking responsibility, in general, means paying attention to only certain aspects of a given situation, which, in turn, allows one to do as one pleases without any pangs of guilt.

A second theme emanating from the story of Cain and Abel underscores interpersonal dynamics. Relationships usually involve close consistent contact and a fair amount of intimacy. Each person experiences the personal strengths and weaknesses of the other.

Relationships as such, don't always provide for an equal exchange of give and take, or for the reflection needed to put things into a proper perspective. People, instead, sometimes take advantage of another's weaknesses or can feel exposed when their own weaknesses become known. Such dynamics appear to be at play between Cain and Abel.

We can detect an imbalance, but we are not given sufficient information as to why such an imbalance exists in the first place. Did Abel's mother or father, or both parents, favor Abel? Was there some developmental (attachment) issue that usurped Cain's ability to fully trust others and to feel adequately secure in his own being? What appears to be obvious is that Abel was a favored individual while Cain was depicted as withholding, taciturn, and moribund.

Cain's predicament is further complicated from a cultural point of view. As the first born, Cain should have been given the place of accession within his family tree, but he was not. Abel, instead, occupied this favored position for reasons that are not clear. Out of that context a competition evolved between these two brothers—a competition to decide who could best please God through the art of sacrifice. As the story unfolds, the reader learns that Abel raises sheep while Cain, a farmer, grows produce. Both apparently work hard and are generally good men.

Within the context of the times, it appears that the sacrifice of a live animal was more precious than the sacrifice of farm produce. Cain's offering was judged to be inferior, even though he may have worked as hard or even harder than Abel.

If Cain's offering had been equally valued, he would have felt blessed and accepted in the eyes of his God, and in turn he would have been able to love himself as well as his brother.

Alter in his commentary on Chapter 4 of Genesis states:

> The widespread culture-founding story of rivalry between herdsman and farmer is recast in a pattern that will dominate Genesis—the displacement of the firstborn by the younger son. If there is any other reason intimated as to why God would favor Abel's offering and not Cain's, it would be in the narrator's stipulation that Abel brings the very best of his flock to God. (2019, 19, 4-5)

Cain, however, is not offering his best. His failure to be more generous results in estrangement and isolation. His mounting anger and envy need a place to go, and it ends up directed at Abel. The mirror image of Abel's goodness gets reflected to Cain as a constant reminder of his own shortcomings and inadequacies.

This biblical story is illustrative of what happens in real life when people are not equal in their capacity to love and be loved. How often is this the presenting problem with those who show up in our consultation rooms?

We might conjecture that Cain had to hold something back in his relationships as a self-protective measure and this, in turn, reduced his chances to succeed. Some people can deal with a sense of failure, perhaps by either lowering their expectations or by taking active steps to improve themselves, while others are haunted by the experience.

Abel, the more loving and the more secure individual, could give fully of himself. Cain was not able to do this. He was apparently riddled with self-doubt and unable to give his very best offering to God. Concomitantly, Cain was also envious of his brother's abilities, and this envy provided an aggressive coloring to Cain's judgment. It was not just the fact that his sacrifice was 'produced from the field. It was more the idea that in his insecurity he had to hold something back. His gift was not a total offering from his heart.

HOLDING SOMETHING BACK

When we hold back something due to our insecurity or because of an old slight or wound, we simply can't give the situation our best effort. Cain was thus unable to participate fully in his sacrifice, and as a result, God, and the world around him responded unfavorably, or certainly with reduced enthusiasm. Abel, on the other hand, received additional blessings. This is simply the way of life and there are no guarantees of fairness across the board. Some people are just more outwardly beautiful, talented, nurtured, accepted, rewarded, and lucky. Some people have a greater capacity to suffer or to supplement their suffering into something useful. Some simply do not have this capacity.

The story of Cain and Abel helps to illuminate the dynamics of how two brothers, when placed in competition with one another, and with different cognitive and emotional abilities, proceed step by step toward a tragic outcome. Without sufficient insight into the causes of Cain's behavior it appears to be largely automatic.

One major purpose of analysis after all is to make the unconscious conscious. With awareness comes the potential to attempt something different and to achieve a better, healthier result.

So why did Cain decide to kill Abel? Abel, I believe, was a constant reminder to Cain of his own deeply felt ineptitude—his lack of internalization of self-worth. There doesn't appear to have been any moderating factors available to Cain to attenuate his agonized face staring back at himself from the mirror. At the most obvious level, the killing was a hateful outburst that provided Cain with a temporary inflation that he desperately needed during a time of personal crisis. He felt upset and angry and full of rage. The murder of Abel helped Cain to reduce his uncomfortable feelings and emotions by giving him a temporary though fraudulent sense of power and ascendency over his brother, a good example of Goodheart's (1980) idea of persona restoration.

We might conjecture that Cain's floundering ego, in association with his "victim complex" and its archetypal energy source, pushed him into an unconscious action, or "acting out."

This is another example of what Goodheart (1980) referred to as a "complex discharging field." But unlike the prepared and trained analyst, Abel doesn't have any idea what's coming his way. If he did, perhaps, he might have been able to contain, to avoid, or to defuse Cain's rage.

Goodheart stated "I conceptualize this field as the person's use of the persona in a defensive manner in order to withdraw from any meaningful or revealing contact with either the analyst or his own inner life." (4) Horney discussed the issue of exploitation of others and thought such behavior served to counteract a sense of inner barrenness. She stated, "When he defeats others, he wins a triumphant elation which obscures his own helpless defeat." (1945, 206-207) The elation Cain obtained, unfortunately, was only short lived. His predicament (or the deeper soul work that he needed to address) did not improve with the death of his brother. It only got worse. But sometimes that is what is needed for the psyche to position itself for potential growth.

BEHAVIORAL REPERTOIRE

... strong impulses are only perilous when not properly balanced; when one set of aims and inclinations is developed into a strength, while others, which ought to coexist with them, remain weak and inactive. It is not because men's desires are strong that they act ill; it is because their consciences are weak.

—MILLS, 1856, 79

A behavioral repertoire is a collection of possible well-rehearsed behaviors available to an individual in meeting the demands of a given situation. It can be likened to a toolbox. When a repair job arises, some individuals will have an abundance of tools to choose from; some will have an adequate supply; others will be woefully lacking in all departments. The individual with the knowledge and right tools will always have an easier time with the task before them. In every case, however, the individual will have a preference about which tool to select first, second, and then third, regardless of whether that tool is the best one for the job. What is important to note is that without adequate resources and the appropriate tools, and the proper temperament, individuals will struggle with the task at hand. In any case, they will work to do their best with the tools that are available to them.

According to Rhodes:

Selves are not given. They are constructed. They are built, modified, altered, refurbished, and even replaced over time. I was a child, but now I'm a man. I was a son, and now I'm also a father and grandfather. I was going to be a preacher, but I became a writer instead. A shy young woman becomes Eleanor Roosevelt, Saul of Tarsus becomes Paul in an over-whelming experience of conversion, a little Indian boy becomes Gandhi, and a child frightened by the sounds of violence from his mother's bedroom becomes a brutal rapist. That selves elaborate across our lives is obvious, but what process inscribes the track of those elaborations remains to be determined, because not every shy young woman becomes a charismatic humanitarian, and not every frightened child becomes a violent criminal. (1999, 55)

Why then do we judge all individuals equally regarding their behavioral controls when in fact all individuals are not equally equipped. Each of our toolboxes is of a different size and has different contents. Not every person's internal dialogue will result in a planning session that says: "If I stay calm right now, I will be able to figure out the best approach to this situation. If I just count to ten, my anger will begin to dissipate." Such planning requires an ability to both see the bigger picture and to assess what is the best course of action prior to opening the tool chest. Such abilities can be enhanced in an individual who has people to reach out to, the wherewithal to reach out to them, and the capacity to benefit from such reaching out.

One way to look at a person's ability to function in any situation is to liken it to a chain of behaviors made up of several stimulus-response links that are closely associated with one another. Each stimulus—response link is both independent from and interdependent upon what has come before it. It has independence because, in theory, there is room between the initial stimulus and the subsequent response within each link for potential reflection and modification. Without reflection, however, each stimulus-response link falls automatically like a domino effect. So, the more habitual the chain, the less likely it is to be modified by reflection. Furthermore, as the individual traverses along the behavioral chain the power of the primary reinforcer increasingly erodes any decision-making ability to reflect and to modify one's behavior. (See Diagram 2 for a visual overview of the Behavioral Chain process.)

All behavior, including the exercise of violence, begins with an initial stimulus, which can be internal or external, (represented by S1) followed by an initial response (represented by R1). What begins as a very small sensation can become the snowball that gains size and speed as it tumbles down the psychological mountainside.

Eventually the size and momentum of a particular behavioral sequence becomes too great to keep it in check. It begins to have a mind of its own, as if seized by a tractor beam, and is now under the full control of the reinforcement or the constituted complex. You can shout from the mountaintops. You can jump up and down like Rumpelstiltskin. You can hold your breath. But the process has been placed on autopilot and come hell or high water the chain will run its course.

It becomes paramount then, that only through early intervention by others, or a conscious decision on the part of the individual, can a person consciously change directions (use his or her other tools) before losing the possibility of self-control as they become more and more under the influence of the reinforcer. Early intervention requires a certain amount of "consciousness" to override what is already reinforced by habit and simply wishes to follow its well-worn path. For example, an addict in recovery sees a movie that he watched with his friends when he was shooting up. This brings back the whole atmosphere, the comradery, the anticipation, the risk, the excitement, He feels lonely and sorry for himself. Sitting at home with nothing to do but watch reruns on TV. He picks up the phone and calls his old dealer, just for old times' sake. And this leads to relapse and such relapses can lead to dire consequences.

I recall a story from an inmate who had a cocaine addiction and several arrests for dealing. He had just gotten out of prison and had gone through a drug treatment program as part of his incarceration. After release from prison, he got together with his best friend to celebrate his freedom. One thing led to the next when his friend stated: Wouldn't it be nice to use cocaine one last time just to mark this occasion? His friend pulled out some cocaine and they started doing lines. In a moment of shock and realization the recently released inmate flew into a rage and strangled his best friend to death for having tempted him to use drugs again, which only represented a return to his old ways and a destruction of his hopes for a better future.

DIAGRAM 2
The Behavioral Chain

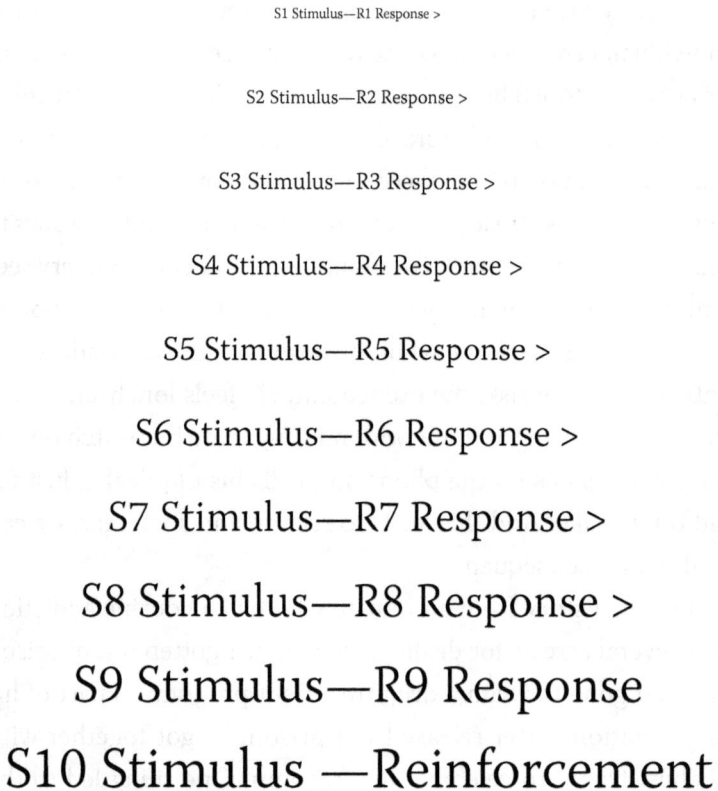

S1 Stimulus—R1 Response >

S2 Stimulus—R2 Response >

S3 Stimulus—R3 Response >

S4 Stimulus—R4 Response >

S5 Stimulus—R5 Response >

S6 Stimulus—R6 Response >

S7 Stimulus—R7 Response >

S8 Stimulus—R8 Response >

S9 Stimulus—R9 Response

S10 Stimulus —Reinforcement

The ability to stay conscious is often referred to as a state of mindfulness. Notice in the visual depiction of the behavioral chain in Diagram 2 that as a person progresses along the chain the font grows bigger. This is to emphasize the increasing power of the primary reinforcer. The closer a person gets to the end of the sequence, the stronger the pull. By the time a person gets to the S5 position they are on autopilot and out of options, and no longer able to exercise any self-control. They are now at the mercy and direction of the addiction, the emotion, or the complex that has been fully energized.

Let it be emphasized again, that a person's behavior is not just a matter of knowing about societal or self-expectations in any given circumstance. It is also not just a matter of the individual's level of psychopathy or how committed the person is to pro-social values. Current need, especially in times of threat and an inundation of stress, will call forth immediate, overlearned behaviors that can and will occur automatically. A conscious choice to inhibit previously lifelong behavior patterns and to replace them with newly learned responses is a tremendous challenge for a person who feels threatened and must respond quickly.

THE EMPIRICAL - BEHAVIORIST TRADITION

Decision becomes an instrumentality of such past reinforcements, so that it is not the decision-making process that is free—the range of alternatives freeing the organism from a singular course of behavior defines freedom.

—RYCHLAK, 1981, 532

Thus, if you have several options available to you when you are forced to decide, you are freer than the individual who has fewer options. I recall working with a prisoner I'll call 'Zeke.' He was describing a conflict with his cellmate and recalled making use of all the cognitive behavioral strategies that he had learned in therapy about how to deal with his mounting anger in a variety of scripted situations.

This had seemed to work well enough under normal conditions when Zeke did not feel overwhelmed, or when the therapist was there to hold his proverbial hand. But on this occasion, after he had experienced several minutes of teasing, back and forth, utilizing his acquired techniques, he found himself out on a vulnerable limb, so to speak.

When his cellmate made a disparaging remark about his mother, that was it. That was the last straw.. All caution was thrown to the winds and only one option remained, namely, to strike out. For this lapse in judgment, Zeke received an additional year on his sentence, and at the time he felt that it was worth it. Zeke's reaction was reminiscent of the old Popeye cartoons in which Popeye is pushed to the brink of his self-control: "That's all I can stand I can't stand no more." For Popeye and Zeke, it's spinach time!

The difference between Popeye and Zeke is that Popeye possesses a much longer emotional fuse and embraced more pro-social attitudes. The more pro-social an individual the more he or she is committed to remaining a citizen in good standing. Individuals with a psychological allergy, or who have an adaptation to the dark, or who are overly sensitive to personal slights and the fear of being disrespected, may eat their spinach almost immediately.

THE FALLACY OF FREE WILL

Once I stood in a desolate square and watched a whole heap of scraps of paper chasing one another. I couldn't feel the wind, as I was in the shelter of a house, but there they were, all chasing each other, murder in their hearts. Next instant they appeared to have decided on an armistice, but all of a sudden, some unendurable puff of bitterness seemed to blow through the lot of them, and off they went again, each hounding on his next door neighbor till they disappeared round the corner. One solid piece of newspaper only lagged behind; it lay helplessly on the pavement, flapping venomously up and down, like a fish out of water, gasping for air. I couldn't help the thought that rose in me: if we, when all's said and done, aren't something similar to these little bits of fluttering paper. Driven hither and thither by some invisible, incomprehensible wind, that dictates our actions, while we in our simplicity think that we have free will.

—Meyrink, 1976, 25

Meyrink's description of the fluttering papers comes very close to my own sense of how much free will most people have. Whenever I share this pessimistic view of humankind, most of my colleagues and friends are taken aback. Free will indicates that an individual has the agency to select and to choose. Without this agency, or an awareness that is compromised by stress, how can there be a true exercise of free will?

When things go well enough, most individuals can handle what's put on their plate. Some individuals have adequate resources (or toolboxes) while other individual's resources are woefully limited.. Yet society holds all individuals to the same level of responsibility.

While it is true that all individuals are ultimately responsible for their actions, those in positions of judgment must consider the background and experience. Without such understanding, how can wise decisions be reached?

In *Memories, Dreams, Reflections,* Jung stated:

In many cases in psychiatry, the patient who comes to us has a story that is not told, and which as a rule no one knows of. To my mind, therapy only begins after the investigation of the wholly personal story. It is the patient's secret, the rock against which he is shattered. (1961, 117)

Behavior is rarely, if ever, simply directed by an act of free will. It has many influencers, many of which are unknown. The known is only the tip of the psychological iceberg.

GOOD AND EVIL INTENT

A symptom suffers most when it does not know where it belongs.

—JAMES HILLMAN, 1999, 189

Human behavior will manifest at various points along a dialectical continuum represented at one end by Evil and at the other end by Good. The reader is free to substitute any pair of opposites in this continuum, and the point I wish to make should still hold true. As a person moves right or left, and away from the center of calm consciousness, he or she will, step by step, fall increasingly under the control of that pole's influence. Going left on the continuum below usurps consciousness with increasing light. Going right consciousness is gradually obliterated with increasing darkness.

GOOD   CONSCIOUSNESS   EVIL

The Middle Path in Action

Returning to my experience working as a freshly minted psychologist in the prison system, I found that my liberal and naïve views about the world did not pass muster. I needed additional education and the ability to keep my eyes wide open. 'Public safety' was and is the primary goal above all others when making decisions about who gets released during the yearly evaluations of an inmate's progress or at the eventual parole hearings.

While others were hunkering down, however, making black and white decisions, and defending themselves against being hoodwinked, I wanted to create a middle place in which to do my job—but with new safeguards built into my psychological attitude. I soon realized that the place that an individual occupies psychologically, even when it is not at the extreme evil pole, it could still be out of reach and beyond our capacity for treatment to change it.

Some individuals, both in prison, as well as in our analytic offices, are simply frozen in place. To think that we can or have reached them in this place of ice could indicate a self-inflation on our part. We may feel momentarily generous and compassionate, but we fall back to earth and smash upon whatever surface awaits us when our judgment has been wrong.

Hillman cautioned:

The descent to the underworld can be distinguished from the night sea journey of the hero in many ways. We have already noticed the main distinction: the hero returns (as Beowulf from his battle with Grendel) from the night sea journey in better shape for the tasks of life, whereas the nekyia takes the soul into the depth for its own sake so that there is no return.

The night sea journey is further marked by building interior heat whereas the *nekyia* goes below that pressured containment, the tempering in the fires of passion to a zone of utter coldness. (1979, 168)

OPTIONS

So what options are open to those of us who attempt to reach dark-adapted individuals? The one path that comes to mind is not for the timid. It demands great patience and fortitude. As the dialectical pendulum swings back and forth within the psyche, the individual is presented with an opportunity, albeit of short duration, to be conscious.

In these fleeting moments, both sides of the continuum can be viewed and reflected upon in a place I call consciousness. Consciousness, to a large degree, represents what Goodheart refers to as the "Secure Symbolizing Field."

Goodheart stated:

This is the field where circumambulation of dream and fantasy, active imagination, non-verbal work with art materials or sand play and clear discussion of transference experiences will occur virtually spontaneously, the patient almost falling into these activities by himself. (1980, 9)

With the support of a guide such as Virgil, or from the safety of the therapeutic vessel, we, the analyst and analysand may glimpse the vestiges of the phenomenon we seek. Words that have been used to describe such a place in various philosophical schools include: consciousness [used in the diagram], individuation, Tao,

---

integration, *coniunctio*, maturity, the magnetic center (Ouspensky, 1949, 201), Gurdjieff's 'Law of Three' (Ouspensky, 1949, 77), insight, emotional growth, and Aristotle's concept of the Golden Mean (1925, 30-31), which in discussing moral behavior he described as the mean between two extremes—at one end is excess, at the other deficiency.

The realization of this process is an arduous task for the individual and therapist alike, and one fraught with a multitude of fears, failures, and questions. With the monsters that we will explore shortly, it will become clearer which of them has a capacity to be conscious and which of them does not.

William James advised:

Different individuals present constitutional differences in this matter of width of field. Your great organizing geniuses are men with habitually vast fields of mental vision, in which a whole program of future operations will appear dotted out at once, the rays shooting far ahead into definite directions of advance. In common people there is never this magnificent inclusive view of a topic. They stumble along, feeling their way, as it were, from point to point, and often stop entirely. In certain diseased conditions consciousness is a mere spark, without memory of the past or thought of the future, and with the present narrowed down to some one simple emotion or sensation of the body. (1902, 198)

WHAT WE CAN EXPECT

Prior to stepping over the threshold into such an enterprise that Jung referred to as an *opus contra naturum* (an act against nature)

---

all possible routes of escape and excuse are likely to present themselves. Sirens will sing their tempting songs with great talent and passion, and tricksters will bark out their advertisements for miracle cures and potions of instant relief. Snake oil and hokum will be the best-selling items in the apothecary, and each of us will have difficulty assessing the merits and flaws of each seductive item. Those who are lighthearted and unprepared will wish to just stay at home, sit on the sofa, and put their feet up and turn on the television, the great pacifier.

Gurdjieff talked about mans' soft underbelly when he stated:

> If there is anything in man able to resist external influences, then this thing itself may also be able to resist the death of the physical body. But think for yourselves what there is to withstand physical death in a man who faints or forgets everything when he cuts his finger.(Ouspensky, 1949, 31-32)

It has recently occurred to me that many of the great figures in history such as Christ, Joan of Arc, Gandhi, Braveheart, Darwin, Thomas Becket, Martin Luther King, Schindler, and Paul Rusesabagina (from the movie *Hotel Rwanda*) had to first get past their fear of death before being able to accept their challenge and fulfill their destinies.

Primal anxiety can freeze us in our tracks and leave us unfulfilled and incomplete. Fear of death can compromise a man's resolve to live fully like no other fear. As Socrates (in Plato's *Phaedo*) muses: "The wise man seeks death throughout his life, and therefore death is not frightening to him." But what percentage of human beings are beyond the fear of death? How many of us would enter the dark willfully as one of my patients did during the following 'active imagination' exercise.

A Patient's Active Imagination in Service of Growth

I left the house from my previous dream for the darkness, not out of any kind of bravado but more for the lack of anything else to live for. I did not care what happened to me because it could not possibly be any worse than my current life. It took a while for anything to happen. I eventually looked back and realized that I was still in the light of the windows of the house in the wilderness. I stepped further away from the lights and into the shadows—deeper into the blackness. Then suddenly the face of a wild, large cat was nose to nose with my own. I could see the glint of its eyes. The pointiness of its ears was like the ears of a Lynx. Then it opened its mouth and swallowed me whole. I cried deeply. I was in what seemed like a long dark tunnel. For some reason it felt like I was inside of a snake. It moved.

Suddenly, I was outside of it again, but I felt the weight of the cat pushing down on my head. I could see myself, or what looked like a fainter self, almost transparent. I called out my name, Faith. This transparent self was now under the earth. It was in a hole or something. I dug this other self out and pulled this version of myself up onto the surface all the time calling out my name as though to wake that me up. It was strange and peaceful to hear my own name in my head.

The weight of the cat on my head took me down again. I did not want to go but I was too scared to fight it. It dragged me into the earth. I could see and feel and smell the soil as I was pushed deeper into it like a worm moving through it. I was consciously afraid that I would suffocate and took a deep breath to be sure that I didn't get too carried away with the vision. The soil turned blacker, and I cried deeper. Then we stopped and it seemed that we had come to a more open space. I decided that I wanted the Creature off my head but fearful that if I reached up it would bite my arms off. I thought: So, what! What did it matter at this point?

Sure enough when I tried to free myself from the cat, it scratched, and clawed, and destroyed my arms and tore me to shreds. But as it did so I became the wild cat. I then clawed my way back up through the dirt.

I reached the surface still wild-eyed and frenzied. All the while, I believe someone, myself, was again calling my name. I saw myself, the pale transparent self, lying there lifeless on the ground—the one that I had previously pulled to the surface to save it. But now, as one with the cat I could not help shredding that lifeless self to bits. And then I was calm. I was still the wild cat, but I was calm.

PART TWO

THE PSYCHOLOGICAL MAKEUP

OF MONSTERS

CHAPTER 4

THE BACKGROUND OF
LITERARY MONSTERS

My psychological creativity comes from the respect I now have for those unredeemable figures of my inferiority feelings. All monsters ask for a chance to evolve, an occasion to appear on stage and react with disgust at fantasies of redemption. What they are asking for is much simpler: to join the living. In exchange, they will do some of the living for us; they love to participate, to play, to write a few chapters in our life stories.

—PARIS, 2007, 78

THE BEHAVIOR OF PSYCHOPATHS, antisocial individuals, psychotics, the mentally ill, and the fanatic has oftentimes been lumped together and understood within a context of superstition, evil, and myth. When bad and inexplicable things occur, people have invented monsters and developed various superstitions as an avenue to understand and manage these superstitions. To feel in control of our darker impulses we have invented extreme methods, such as burning witches at the stake, and other forms of torture, to corral or project the darker aspects of our human existence.

In truth, the many monsters that have been created and the ones that will be explored in this book, namely *Frankenstein*, *Dracula*, *The Phantom of the Opera*, *The Werewolf*, *The Strange Case of Dr. Jekyll and Mr. Hyde*, *The Pied Piper*, *The Golem*, and *Dorian Gray*, did not come from outer space or from one of the levels of Dante's *Inferno*. Instead, they were born in our own homes, next door, or just down the street.

Writers of fiction such as Gaston Leroux, Mary Shelly, Robert Lewis Stevenson, Oscar Wide, and Bram Stoker have written captivating stories that, in essence, look deeply into the sub-strata of our human motivation. And because these stories are archetypal and the stuff of myth, they seem to stay alive and remain informative to each subsequent generation of readers.

According to Early "It is the hallmark of archetypal literature that a story becomes identified by itself and not as having been written by anyone in particular." (1983, 34) Each story illustrates to some degree an aspect of ourselves that we would rather avoid, ignore, or disown. Themes of abandonment, power, control, beauty, ugliness, revenge, and pride will guide the reader to experience epiphanies of operatic proportions if readers are brave enough to take a closer, deeper look.

Such stories can reconnect us to those parts of ourselves that have been suppressed and hidden. And, as we examine these themes more closely, we will likely find that the etiology of such behaviors, even though they may disturb us to the core, become more understandable.

Baumeister advises us "understanding evil begins with the realization that we ourselves are capable of doing many of these things." (1997, 5) This has certainly been my experience, and I have been humbled by it. Is there any other realization more disquieting than the possibility that a monster exists in each one of us, a monster that can lie dormant and unassembled?

All that said, it is hoped that the reader will be persuaded that being bad is not always the product of Evil, per se. The corollary can also be true: Being good is not always the product of moral upbringing and the adherence to one's scruples. Oftentimes, instead, it is more the by-product of several complicated ingredients, usually related to a specific context, some of which we have control over, when we are wide awake and prepared to act, with the required skills to make the necessary adjustments, and some of which we appear ignorant about and do not have any control over. As my first analyst KJ would always say: "We are asleep most of the time."

It is my hope that you, the reader, will gain an increasing ability to differentiate between the antisocial and the psychopathic individual, both of whom operate from somewhat different places along the continuum of Good and Evil.

The antisocial has more potential to adjust to the lighter side of the Continuum whereas the Psychopath seems frozen and to have no potential. The reader may also wish to find his or her own place on the continuum in the safety of his or her own private thoughts. Being able to make such distinctions is an important task, especially for those of us who will be asked to decide such things as: Who is evil? Who is sick? Who should receive treatment? Who will benefit or has benefitted from treatment? Who is ready to be returned to the community at large and who should perhaps remain safely locked away inside the container called prison? All these issues pertain directly to the overall safety of our society and may decide who lives down the street from us in the future.

Finally, I wish to state that my thoughts, ideas, and findings are not meant to excuse violence, or criminal behavior in its widest definition. Such behavior must be met and countered with the most tenacious and containing responses available to us. Such responses should be geared first at maintaining the safety of society and its people. Many of the characters discussed in this book, even if therapeutically treatable, may need to remain in an institution separated from society for the longest possible period.

CHAPTER 5

FRANKENSTEIN

The Quest for Justice through the Act of Revenge

PCL-R Scores
Victor Frankenstein 7, the Creature 3. Non-criminal range

Shall I respect man when he condemns me? Let him live with me in the interchange of kindness, and instead of injury I would bestow every benefit upon him with tears of gratitude at his acceptance. But that cannot be. The human senses are insurmountable barriers to our union. Yet mine shall not be the submission of abject slavery. I will avenge my injuries; if I cannot inspire love, I will cause fear, and chiefly towards you my archenemy, because my creator, do I swear inextinguishable hatred. Have a care; I will work at your destruction, nor finish until I desolate your heart, so that you shall curse the hour of your birth.

—MARY SHELLY, 1816/1992, 146-147, CH.17

MARY SHELLY'S (1816/1992) *Frankenstein* is the first of seven literary figures that I will explore in detail to locate each character's place along the heretofore described continuum of

Good and Evil. Her story includes a myriad of the themes that typify life, but it is not a narrative that ends in '… and they all lived happily ever after.' Shelly, to her non-Disney like credit, was not trying to keep us from the darker aspects of our human nature.

On the contrary, she apparently set out to tell a tale of regress to shed light on the darker aspects of our shared humanity. Instead of things getting better, they keep getting worse. The story takes us gradually and sequentially into a cul-de-sac that leads to the dark at the end of the tunnel —not to an opening onto the other side of the mountain.

Instead of improving upon our humanity the story takes us backward into a chaos of its own making. And yet, despite this chaos, there remains an ever-present smidgen of hope, on the periphery, suggesting that something may yet emerge which can transform the tragic into something merciful, something better. That hope, in essence, is what provides both the story and our species with the courage to believe in the possibility of change and human evolvement, despite so much evidence to the contrary.

Approached from a psychodynamic point of view, Shelly's saga concerns the ego's attempt to deny the 'way of all flesh' by exhibiting a ubiquitous desire to reign over and to control everything that can challenge or injure it. The ego accomplishes this by using manic defenses of Herculean proportions, employed to protect Victor from what he, and all humans fear most, death.

The idea of manic defenses originated with Melanie Klein (1940) when she sought to extend Freud's theory regarding manic depressive illness. She observed that when the ego is under pressure it sometimes employs a manic defense whereby it attempts to reassert its control by denying the troubling parts of reality by replacing them with a sense of invincibility.

Such a defense can be exemplified by a phrase that I often voiced to my son, during his formulative years, namely, "You can't hurt steel." I would use this cliché whenever my son would punch me in the arm in a playful manner. Via this phrase I would subtly reduce my own Oedipal fears, reassure myself of my own strength, and then have it further reinforced by the notion that my son would see me as Superman.

I imagine that soldiers facing death in battle sometimes employ the same type of mind defense to steel their nerves and do what they must do. Otherwise, they might be engulfed by their fear of death. Fanatics, as well, such as suicide bombers, are likely to embrace the delusional belief that they will be immediately transported to heaven or some other paradise as a reward for their sacrifice.

Melanie Klein felt that these "manic defenses were largely "typified" by three feelings: control, triumph, and contempt. In Victor Frankenstein's failure to come to terms with the fact that all life dies, he seeks to supersede the mystery of death and to render it null and void. He, of course, is not the first, nor will he be the last to attempt such folly.

Death has never been an easy reality to accept for any individual. When placed in its proper perspective, however it can be the ingredient that supplies life with its deeper richness and its fuller meaning. Its denial, on the other hand, only serves to truncate human wholeness.

The central Creature in Shelley's story is thus birthed out of Dr. Frankenstein's fanatical desire to create and control life.

At the death of his mother, when Victor is seventeen, he is left bereft and ill prepared to manage life as an independent, autonomous adult. He is still too dependent on his mother's love and guidance. Overwhelmed by such an abrupt emotional severance Victor wishes to cleave to the ever-providing, though now absent maternal breast—and finds himself unable to face and to integrate death's profound significance.

In despair, Victor retreats into the laboratory to research and experiment with the secrets of bestowing life upon the inanimate. While the problem may have been manageable, heretofore, if faced in its infancy and with the help of others who love him, including his fiancé and his father, it now begins to compound itself.

Victor, with the assistance of his manic defenses, and not the healthy support from others, as he chooses to isolate himself, endeavors to reach the realm of the gods and to hold within his own hands the ability to defeat death by discovering its antidote. By defeating death, the foundation of all anxiety (Becker, 1973), Victor hopes to eliminate mankind's primal vulnerability.

Like Thetis in her attempt to immortalize and protect Achilles from human frailty, fate and reality always find a way to remind us that we are not gods. (Cotterell and Storm, 2003, 14) The ankle of Achilles would remain vulnerable to the piercing of an arrow despite his prowess as a warrior, and Victor Frankenstein will also face a penalty for ignoring the dictates of the natural order.

Dr. Frankenstein declares his intentions:

No one can conceive the variety of feelings, which bore me onwards, like a hurricane, in the first enthusiasm of success. Life and death appeared to me ideal bound, which I should first break through, and pour a torrent of light into our dark world. A new species would bless me as its creator and source; many happy and excellent natures would owe their being to me. (46)

In such a plan, Victor Frankenstein now exhibits the manic defenses of hubris and grandiosity, in addition to the Kleinian concepts of control and triumph. These traits, each, by itself, or in combination, always attract their own brand of comeuppance. For when men and women seek to act as gods, especially for their own selfish or deluded purposes, like Icarus seduced to fly too high despite the instructions and warnings of his father Daedalus, the action always goes awry and crashes back to earth.

There is a price to be paid and the correction of one-sidedness is brought back into balance by the archetypal commandment: Thou shall be whole! And that is what Dr. Frankenstein has put into motion.

By attempting to eradicate death and by refusing to integrate the loss of his mother into himself, as a part of the wholeness of life, he has unwittingly set himself up to create the Creature that will now require him to come to terms with the very same things he has wished to avoid. And the Creature will embody and play its role to perfection. The Creature will ultimately force Victor Frankenstein to face the human reality of loss, separation, mortality, and death. And this will all come at a great cost.

A KINDRED SPIRIT

Interestingly, Shelly begins her story by introducing Captain Walton's letter home to his sister concerning the "kindred spirit" that he has encountered on his journey of discovery. With Walton, we are being presented with evidence, although maybe at first not self-evident, that Victor Frankenstein's predicament isn't simply an outlier. Perhaps, instead, this desire to visit the land of the gods may be a ubiquitous trait in human beings.

In Walton's case, a kindred spirit referred to another man, like himself, who seeks to find something that will set him apart from other men, and act to assure his place in history. Is this not a way to defeat death and to achieve immortality? Yes!

Both men seem ill content with being mere mortals. They strive to make their mark on the world and to be remembered for something large. It is not enough to simply to be a father, a husband, a worker, or a commoner. Frankenstein and Walton both attempt to reach beyond the mundane to avoid the usual anxieties present in all lives. But, as we will see, this only results in another set of problems and obstacles that leads back to what was not faced in the first place.

Striving to do something heroic, in and of itself, can be admirable, but if it is just done to glorify oneself, it is likely done to protect the ego from fear and anxiety, and not to face fear or to benefit humankind. This represents a contrast between individualism (ego-centered) and the Jungian concept of individuation (ego-Self balance).

Dr. Frankenstein, unfortunately, doesn't directly face what he fears. He looks instead for ways to soothe his venerable ego. In his quest to create life, Victor's creation is flawed from the very beginning because he has been blind to something essential. The Creature, you may remember, is composed of the body parts of various dead people, parts that have been sawed and stitched, desecrated, and discarded. And while the Creature is a whole being in the figurative sense, for it had all the limbs and things that outwardly comprise a human being, these things are not, by subjective nature, it's things. They do not work together as a "whole" because they have not arrived at this juncture in time through a natural developmental process which, through steps, has resulted in an integrated whole. Forcing parts together cannot produce an authentic organic whole being, and that is what Victor Frankenstein has failed to comprehend.

Shelly, interestingly, does not actually address this issue of "disparate parts" in her story. Venables (1980), however, in his book about *Frankenstein*, does a good job of thinking through this conundrum. In *The Frankenstein Diaries*, Venable presents his own fictional account of Dr. Frankenstein in a similar manner that Orson Wells presented his radio show in 1938, featuring H.G. Well's "The War of the Worlds."

I must admit, with some confession of naïveté, that at first, and for some time, as I was reading, I was mesmerized by this book and even thought, much like Well's radio audience, that it might not be fiction but real. When I had picked up the book initially, I read the following:

"Unknown to fiction writers from Mary Shelly to the screenwriters of Hollywood, the personal diaries and papers of Viktor Frankenstein, creator of living beings, lay untouched and forgotten for over 150 years." [inside cover]

In Venable's book, Frankenstein discovers during his initial experiments that the various body parts he has assembled are not knitting together but are acting like independent entities. The greater part of the anatomy, meaning the part of the Creature that is, to a large extent, one body part, steadfastly refuses to be associated with the superficial, added members, and "the common sutures are already showing signs of atrophy. Each section, for example, the limbs, appears to be drawing into itself. (58)

Frankenstein later makes the following observation after he is awakened at night by a "shrieking of such a terrifying nature that I felt the blood stand still in my veins." (Venables, 1980, 63)

Victor observed:

I spent the day wondering in the forest trying to ascertain what had been the cause of the tragedy and have concluded that even a dead brain retains a physical or chemical impression of identity. Somehow the young man who had perished in the Wurzburg hospital had been revived in the stimulated tissue. Though I find it hard to conceive, I must have inadvertently resurrected the soul of the dead man! That dreadful sound persists in my mind, and I am unsettled by the thought of the agonies that his soul, or whatever entity it may have been, must have suffered at being brought back from the dark realm of Death to such circumstances. It is as though it were indeed the voice of hell.(65)

How different Frankenstein's creation turns out to be from that of God, the supreme creator, who it is said, created humankind in his own image. As a result of being created in God's image, some cultures have held the belief that they hold a special place in the hierarchy of living things, a position giving them dominion over all other creatures.

Beginning at such a place of distinction is, in and of itself, comforting. Such comfort provides confidence and an archetypal springboard (an élan vital) into all subsequent creative outputs. This belief provides a positive aspect of narcissism which is needed in almost any challenging pursuit. Most importantly, however, after God created man and woman, he reviewed his work and said: "It is good."

Simply put, the original creator basked in the glory of his achievement, and this glory was further reflected positively in all subsequent creations. Having value, it appears, both in one's own eyes as well as in the eyes of others, can provide an elixir of well-being.

But as we shall see in the story of Frankenstein, not all creators can control their creations. There may even be enough evidence to suggest, though it cannot be investigated in this book, that not even the gods have such ability. It seems, however, that anything less than perfection requires flexibility on the part of us all in the form of patience, tolerance, kindness, and charity.

ANIMATION

After the Creature comes to life, Dr. Frankenstein is shocked and appalled at what he has created. Instead of looking upon his creation with a creator's ardor and enthusiasm, he experiences just the opposite, specifically the negative shadowy emotions of shame and hatred.

Instead of a sense of achievement, he feels horror and revulsion. He is overcome with anxiety, the very opposite of what he had sought to avoid in the first place. In his disconcertedness, he abdicates any responsibility for his creation and runs away without any thought as to the consequences of what he has done and what will yet transpire.

There has been no forethought as to what the Creature will think, and feel, and how it will behave. Frankenstein acts like an eighteen-year-old adolescent boy who has gotten his girlfriend pregnant and then wants to abdicate all involvement. He runs away and attempts to erase all signs of his folly or demands that his girlfriend get an abortion.

All the while, the newly created Creature, like a child, needs to be fed and cared for. Like most fantasies or ill-conceived plans, Frankenstein has simply assumed from the start that his creation would be good. His quest for fame has blinded his vision.

His naïveté has interfered with thorough planning. Instead of feeling a heightened sense of responsibility, Dr. Frankenstein is thrown into a dark pit of self-doubt and shame because he has not prepared himself for all contingencies. How could he have so planned when his ill-conceived conscious design avoided certain realities? He wanted to hide himself as Adam hid himself in the Garden of Eden. He is subsequently horrified by his creation, and so he rejects it.

Dr. Frankenstein states:

> Oh! No mortal could support the horror of that countenance. A mummy again endured with animation could not be so hideous as that wretch. I had gazed on him while unfinished; he was ugly then, but when those muscles and joints were rendered capable of motion, it became a thing such as even Dante could not have conceived. I passed the night wretchedly. Sometimes my pulse beat so quickly and hardly that I felt the palpitation of every artery; at others, I nearly sank to the ground through languor and extreme weakness. Mingled with this horror, I felt the bitterness of disappointment; dreams that had been my food and pleasant rest for so long a space were now become a hell to me; and the change was so rapid, the overthrow so complete! (51-52)

The Doctor has hastily joined body parts together without considering that a living creature first requires the on-going love and support usually afforded to new creations (young babies and growing children). In the process of natural conception, it is the co-mingling contribution of both the male and the female that begins the gradual development that takes place over time and includes enough nurturance, support, and protection that, in turn, produces a healthy human being.

Dr. Frankenstein has skipped over these vital steps and now wishes that this nightmare of his own making will simply go away. Both Creature and Creator are abysmally prepared to function in the same world together, not because of any inability on the part of the Creature, but solely because Dr. Frankenstein and human-kind cannot find it in themselves to love both the acceptable as well as the abhorrent.

It's as if the Creature represents the darker and most unexplored parts of Victor Frankenstein's psyche, namely, the parts he most wants to deny. The Creature is thus a repository for Victor's shadow, a shadow he has rejected.

Psychological development, however, is comprised of essential, experiential building blocks that an infant makes use of in his or her progression toward adulthood. Winnicott 's instructive phrase, "good enough caretaker," is a constant reminder that certain things must be provided to help the child to develop into a "healthy" individual. Borden wrote:

Winnicott realizes that environments are never ideal, but he emphasizes that they must be good enough to facilitate that maturational process. If they are not, he theorizes development is undermined and individuals are at risk for psychopathology, dysfunction, and problems in living; he speaks of a 'freezing of the failure situation' that arrests the development of the self. (2009, 93)

When these "good enough" things are largely absent, certain difficulties, as I have mentioned earlier, are likely to manifest.

The Creature begins life as an outcast, estranged from himself and others. He discovers his identity slowly, as we all do, through interactions with the external environment. However, instead of experiencing acceptance and unconditional love, he experiences repeated rejection, first at the hands of his creator and then subsequently by everyone he meets.

There is nothing that approaches the threshold of being 'good enough.' The Creature is simply alone. People are repulsed and frightened by his grotesque and strange appearance. Instead of building a good sense of self, based on positive interchanges with others, he grows to see himself as a monster. Unlike Narcissus, who falls in love with his own reflection (Cotterell & Storm, 2003, 65), the Creature is repulsed by what he sees staring back at him. The Creature states:

> Increase of knowledge only discovered to me more clearly what a wretched outcast I was. I cherished hope, it is true, but it vanished when I beheld my person reflected in water or my shadow in the moonshine, even as that frail image and that inconstant shade. (131)

Where there had been the potential to be more fully human there was now a growing sense of injustice and a concomitant desire to seek revenge against his creator, the one who had placed him in such an untenable position to begin with.

The Creature states:

> All save I, were at rest or enjoyment; I, like the archfiend, bore

---

Dr. Frankenstein's Creature

a hell within me, and finding myself un-sympathized with, wished to tear up the trees, spread havoc and destruction around me, and then to have sat down and enjoyed the ruin. But this was a luxury of sensation that could not endure; I became fatigued with excess of bodily exertion and sank on the damp grass in the sick impotence of despair. There were none among the myriads of men that existed who would pity or assist me; and should I feel kindness towards my enemies? No; from that moment I declared everlasting war against the species, and more than all, against him who had formed me and sent me forth to this insupportable misery. (136)

What is most important to note here is that the Creature did not automatically become a monster. Monsterhood was a process that developed over the course of time and followed multiple setbacks and disappointments.

Initially, the Creature had attempted to learn the ways of humankind. He had assumed himself to be human. After all, his creator was a human being. He studied language and learned to speak from listening to others. During times of loneliness, he was warmed by the thought of human love and friendship, which he had read about in books. He believed in what he had read, and he worked to forge a connection with others.

He was a potential pro-social being at this point. He was still attracted to the lighter side of the Adaptation Continuum. He wanted to show that he, too, had something valuable to offer. He carried out acts of kindness that demonstrated an empathic connection to the needs of others. One such example of kindness was his gathering of wood for the family who live in the cottage on the edge of the forest. He was pleased that his surreptitious actions were appreciated. He thus began to foster an ideal image of others and to fantasize about possible successful interactions. After reading *Paradise Lost* (Milton, 2004) he began to believe in the concept of salvation, not just in the afterlife but, more importantly, in his present life.

Such points of reference provided him with a psychological lift and a salve to soften his sense of isolation. For a period, he developed faith and a growing sense of naïve optimism. This faith and optimism are even given a chance for realization when he plans his encounter with the blind old man who will not be repulsed by his ugliness. He has intuited that this might be his only opportunity to contact another being without the interference of prejudice and pre-conceived notions of beauty. He has planned to make this attempt while the blind man's family is away on errands in the nearby village. This encounter represents the possibility for a positive life-changing encounter that can prevent a person from proceeding along and completing the Dark Adaptation process.

FAILURE

The Creature's efforts for a positive encounter with the old man prove to be in vain. The blind man's family return abruptly and unexpectedly from their short trip, encountered the Creature, and chase him off. The Creature, thereby, experiences additional despair, which only adds to his already copious supply of previous rejections. He becomes forlorn, dejected, increasingly lonely, and above all else, angry. His desire to be a part of the human family is further dashed and vociferously rejected.

This process has not occurred over night. Its roots, like the meal in a slow cooker, are becoming firmly established in the soil of his existence—through experience. While he has not willingly given into this dark foreboding attitude, he is becoming ever more adapted to the dark. Despite this fact, the Creature states: "If any being felt emotions of benevolence towards me, I should return them a hundred and a hundred-fold, for that one Creature's sake I would make peace with the whole kind." (147)

His antisocial orientation is thus born out of his growing sense of being treated unfairly. It is not a conclusion that he has sought, nor one that he would have preferred. It is nonetheless what has come into being. The Creature begins to experience the goodness and joy of others, not as something any longer within his grasp, but rather as the true cause of his own misery.

In the end, the self-adjudged, justifiable revenge that he seeks, usurps his desire for love and acceptance and flips itself over into hate and rejection. Revenge becomes his guiding principle and represents his only perceived avenue to obtain justice.

How many individuals, in the real world, are forced into similar struggles and forge similar solutions? I am certain that the number is quite large.

FIRST VICTIM

The Creature traveled a long, long distance to extract revenge. Arriving in the woods not far from the Doctor's family estate, the Creature encounters William, Victor's youngest brother. William is taken aback by the Creature's ugliness and attempts to flee. This ignites the Creature's rage at yet another rejection. William further wounds and enrages the Creature when he calls him an ogre. William then exclaims that his "papa" is M. Frankenstein, and that his papa will punish the Creature if it doesn't let William go. This is the final straw. The Creature's anger erupts, and his thirst for revenge explodes with a volcanic force. The Creature states: "Frankenstein! You belong then to my enemy—to him toward whom I have sworn eternal revenge: you shall be my first victim." (143) He then proceeds to strangle the helpless child.

The Creature's next criminal act begins to take shape almost immediately as he bends over the dead child. He notices a beautiful broach with a picture around the boy's neck, and he takes it off the dead child. As he examines it, he states:

> I took it; it was a portrait of a most lovely woman. Despite my malignity, it softened and attracted me. For a few moments I gazed with delight on her dark eyes, fringed with deep lashes, and her lovely lips; but presently my rage returned; I remembered that I was forever deprived of the delights that such beautiful Creatures could bestow and that she whose resemblance I contemplated would, in regarding me, have changed that air of divine benignity to one expressive of disgust and affright." (143)

In the meantime, Justine, the caretaker of the child, has been out searching for William. She is a caring individual with genuine concern for William's welfare. She has grown tired from searching, stops to rest a while, and has innocently fallen asleep. The Creature, in his meanderings, happens upon her. Justine, like the picture of the woman inside the broach, further fuels the Creature's rage. He is reminded that things of beauty and comfort have not been offered to him. His need for revenge hatches the most diabolical of plans. While Justine sleeps the Creature places the broach around her neck. In doing so the Creature hopes that this innocent woman will be implicated and punished for the murder that he has just committed. The idea that the innocent will be blamed and punished is something that the Creature relishes. In essence, his on-going experience of injustice, which he has had to endure, time and time again, will now be shared with Justine. He will no longer be alone in his misery. Someone else will experience what he has had to experience. He too is an innocent but there has been no one willing to hear his cry or to soothe his pain. And his plan works to perfection. Justine is accused, convicted, and executed for the crime she did not commit. No one will step forward to save her. The evidence is too condemning.

While this act is one of unmitigated malice, the Creature continues to have the capacity to reverse course. He has not yet succumbed completely to the Dark Adaptive process. He still longs for a way to live in peace, and he still hungers for relationship.

THE DEVIANT AND THE RECLUSE

The Creature was not an individual born into the human family in the ordinary sense of the word. He was not nurtured through the early stages of human development with love, the support of family, or protection from fear. Instead, he faced an existence ill-equipped to deal with the demands of human existence and societal expectation.

Many human beings experience this same kind of impoverished environment. They too are ill-equipped to engage in social intercourse and to make the contributions to society which would reward them with purpose and acceptance. Some children simply represent a burden to their parents who cannot care for their own rudimentary needs. Instead of succor, these children experience poverty, violence, starvation, neglect, and physical and sexual abuse. Ill-equipped to be part of society they make plans to exercise what few possibilities that are left to them. Two dominant lifestyle options include the deviant and the recluse.

The deviant will operate outside the usual structure and rules that apply to the general populace because they are not accepted into that structure. They take on an attitude of "you have to do whatever is needed to survive." The recluse, on the other hand, chooses on their own to stay outside the structure. Each choice, however, does not yet suggest that either will inevitably be evil or rotten to the core. It only predicts that such a person's behavior will be different in some noticeable way from the 'normal.'

Both Doctor Frankenstein and the Creature still have the theoretical potential to grow and to become more whole. That is why, in a reflective moment, the Creature importunes Dr. Frankenstein to create a female companion for him. Having a companion will reduce the Creature's sense of loneliness, isolation, and rejection, the same factors that fuel his rage and desire for revenge. The Creature states: "No Eve soothed my sorrows nor shared my thought: I was alone. I remembered Adam's supplication to his creator. But where was mine. He had abandoned me. And in the bitterness of my heart, I cursed him." (131)

The Doctor is moved by the Creature's entreaties and considers making the Creature a mate. In the end, however, he decides against such a solution. He is afraid that this will just compound his mistake and bring additional death and destruction. In response to Dr. Frankenstein's refusal the Creature states:

Shall each man find a wife for his bosom, and each beast have his mate, and I be alone? I had feelings of affection, and they were requited by detestation and scorn. Man! You may hate; but beware! Your hours will pass in dread and misery, and soon the bolt will fall which must ravish from you your happiness forever. Are you to be happy while I grovel in the intensity of my wretchedness? You can blast my other passions, but revenge remains—revenge, henceforth dearer than light or food! I may die; but first you, my tyrant and tormentor, shall curse the sun that gazes on your misery. Beware; for I am fearless, and therefore powerful. I will watch with the wiliness of a snake, that I may sting with its venom. Man, you shall repent the injuries you inflict. (188-189)

In a rage the Creature promises to visit Dr. Frankenstein on his wedding night and despite all precautions on the part of the Doctor, he manages to do so. He murders Victor's bride and then escapes with Victor in pursuit. He has sated his need for revenge.

Now both Creature and Creator share parallel experiences of despair. And unfortunately for all, the story ends in the destruction of both the Doctor and the Creature without any further transformation.

Throughout the telling of the story, however, there is always a legitimate reason to hope. The Creature, you see, is simply crying out to be understood and accepted and cared for. In fact, the ending of the tale suggests a conclusion of hostilities, as the need for revenge is exhausted and spent. The Creature destroys himself instead of doing additional harm.

CHAPTER 6

DRACULA

The Vampire as Prototype for the Psychopath

PCL-R score = 32, Highly psychopathic

I was born with the devil in me. I could not help the fact that I was a murderer, no more than the poet can help the inspiration to sing.

—H.H. HOLMES in: *DEVIL IN THE WHITE CITY*
—LARKIN, 2003, 109

Welcome the coming, speed the parting guest.[1]

—STOKER, 1897/2005, 56

---

1 This is the English saying of which Dracula is fond. It is most apropos for vampires and psychopaths. It allows time for the quick objective (like sucking the blood from another) but no place for the deeper development of intimacy.

Dracula

THE VAMPIRE IN BRAM Stoker's *Dracula* is a totally dark-adapted individual. He cannot exist in the light of the sun and must return to the safety of the tomb during the hours of daylight. This vampire, and all vampires, survive only through the consumption of human blood (metaphorically speaking in present day terms). In addition, Dracula has no capacity to feel remorse or guilt because such sentiments only put him at risk for extinction and work in opposition to his primary directive, survival. In clinical terms, he is the quintessential antisocial being, or the psychopath represented at the extreme right end of the Dark Adaptation Continuum.

According to the Publisher's Preface (Stoker, 1897/2005), "Dracula, in the Wallachian language, means devil." (vi) He is the being that looks human to the unsuspecting eye but possesses no essential human qualities once the persona of his humanity is stripped away. Dracula has only one purpose and that is to get his needs met, always at the expense of others. He is a parasite who needs a host to feed upon. He will say and do anything to achieve his objectives and to control a situation. The following three sketches depict the psychopath and the vampire quite accurately in simple language.

SKETCH ONE

A little girl is walking along a cold mountain path covered with snow when she encounters a poisonous snake. Since the snake is a cold-blooded Creature, it is unable to move due to the cold conditions. It is able, however, to ask the girl for assistance.

It entreats: "Little girl, please take me down the mountainside to a place where it is warmer."

The little girl replies: "I will not pick you up and take you down the mountainside where it is warm because you will then bite me."

The snake replies: "Oh no, I won't bite you. I will only be grateful that you have been so kind and have provided me with assistance."

The little girl, as a good feeling human being, then decides to be kind and she picks the snake up and carries him down the mountainside to where it is warm. The snake immediately bites her in the arm.

The girl cries out: "Why did you bite me? You promised me that you wouldn't!"

The snake replies: "Little girl, what did you expect from me? I am a snake!"

SKETCH TWO

There were two squirrels living in the back yard of a little boy's house. One squirrel was collecting acorns from under the big oak and storing them in a safe place. The little boy asked the industrious squirrel what he was doing, and the squirrel replied, "It will be winter soon, and I must make sure that I have enough to eat for me and my family—so I am collecting as many nuts as possible so that we will have an ample supply when it gets cold, and the food supply would otherwise be exhausted."

"Oh, said the boy, you are very wise."

The little boy then became curious about the other squirrel that was apparently just lounging about and didn't seem to be concerned about the coming cold or the food supply. The little boy decided to ask the second squirrel why he wasn't gathering acorns.

The second squirrel replied: "Why should I work so hard. When I get hungry, I will simply hit that other squirrel over the head and take his nuts for my own."

SKETCH THREE

A scorpion approached a body of water and needed to get to the other side. He asked a frog, sitting on the riverbank, if he would be kind enough to carry him across the water. The frog, of course, out of a built-in natural defensive intuition, expressed his concern that the scorpion would sting him if he agreed to such an arrangement. The scorpion replied that he would not be inclined to sting the frog because then they would both drown. Appreciating the scorpion's reasoning, since it did sound reasonable, the frog, out of kindness, agreed to carry the scorpion across the body of water, but halfway across the scorpion stung the frog, and they both drowned. (This underscores the deviousness, untrustworthiness, as well as the impulsivity of the psychopath).

Dracula's parasitic tendencies are on display early during the scene in which Jonathan Harker discovers a library full of English books on a variety of subjects in Dracula's castle. When Harker asks Dracula about this collection, Dracula responds by stating:

> I am glad you found your way in here, for I am sure that there is much that will interest you. These friends—and he laid his hand on some of the books—have been good friends to me, and for some years past, ever since I had the idea of going to London, have given me many, many hours of pleasure. Through them I have come to know your great England; and to know her is to love her. I long to go through the crowded

streets of your mighty London, to be in the midst of the whirl and rush of humanity, to share its life, its change, its death, and all that makes it what it is. But alas! As yet, I only know your tongue through books. To you my friend, I look that I know it to speak. (Stoker, 2005, 23-24)

What Harker doesn't know, at this point, is that Dracula is a vampire and that his move to London is predicated on the instinctual need for a supply of fresh blood. Dracula himself has grown less energetic and older in recent years because the place where he lives, Transylvania, does not supply him with a steady and sufficient stream of victims, only the occasional passerby near his castle in the deep woods. Thus, not unlike the street beggar or the traveling salesman, Dracula must find a place where there is more action, more blood.

What Harker begins to sense, however, is that something just doesn't add up during his exchange with Dracula. Something is awry. There is a cognitive dissonance at play. His consciousness is disturbed by an element not yet identified but attempting to make its presence known. Even before he meets Dracula in person Harker has commented about his sleep during his first night in the Carpathian Mountains during his journey to meet Dracula.:

"I did not sleep well, though my bed was comfortable enough, for I had all sorts of queer dreams. There was a dog howling all night long under my window, which may have had something to do with it, or it may have been the paprika, for I had to drink up all the water in my carafe and was still thirsty." (4)

Harker, like many individuals, sees dreams as something caused by food (too much paprika) or the bark of a dog rather than as a message from the unconscious alerting him that something needs attention.

In addition to his dreams, Harker is also taken aback by the behavior and actions of the people he meets on his way to Dracula's castle. They are all 'afraid' in some unspecified way and appear worried about his welfare. But like his apprehensions in the dream, he does not understand the gravity of their worry or the threat that he is about to face. Despite the many warning signs, he is not yet able to comprehend them. He is like a fly going blindly into the spider's web or the stereotypical naïve blond female star in a "B" movie walking down a dark street at 3 am and just up ahead is a monster ready to jump out and grab her. The movie's musical score is beginning to get agitated, and the moviegoers are all stirring in their seats, but the naïve female character continues to be oblivious to any of this.

A potential victim's non-observation and naïveté is always part and parcel to the psychopath's plan. In fact, the psychopath, and the vampire count on their prey's lack of consciousness and their inability to put all the potential facts and observations together, especially those that don't quite fit. We will see this strategy of psychological subterfuge being implemented and employed by Dracula throughout the story.

Very early into Harker's ordeal with Dracula, Harker starts to sense Dracula's growing hold over him. His anxiety becomes very palpable when the Count requests that Harker remain with him for a full month despite Harker's desire to leave for London ex post haste. Harker resigns himself to this fate, however, since he had been instructed by his superiors back in England to take every care of all the Count's wishes. Harker states

What could I do but bow acceptance? It was Mr. Hawkins' interest and not mine, and I had to think of him, not myself; and besides, while Count Dracula was speaking, there was that in his eyes and in his bearing which made me remember that I was a prisoner, and that if I wished it, I could have no choice. The Count saw his victory in my bow, and his mastery in the trouble of my face, for he began at once to use them, but in his own smooth, restless way. (37)

Harker is succumbing more and more to the mesmerizing control of Dracula, who, in Jungian terms, represents an archetypal energy that has usurped the ability of Harker's ego to make sound judgments and grounded decisions. Harker states:

I am surely in the toils. Last night the Count asked me in the suavest tones to write three letters, one saying that my work here was nearly done, another that I was starting on the next morning from the time of the letter, and the third that I had left the castle and arrived at Bistritz. I would fain have rebelled but felt that in the present state of things it would be madness to quarrel openly with the Count whilst I am so absolutely in his power; and to refuse would be to excite his suspicion and to arouse his anger. (47)

The Count's control over Harker reminds me of an encounter that I had when I was 18 years old. I was living and working at the ocean during the summer break from college and was visiting someone at their boarding house where several restaurant employees lived. A tall, handsome man walked into the area where I was sitting with my friend and gestured to me to follow him. Without thought I stood up and followed him out of the room and down the hall to another room—automatically. He asked me to sit on the bed and then left the room. After several seconds my reasoning ability returned, and I stood up and left the room and returned to where my friend and others were sitting. No one seemed to either notice or comment about my absence.

A few minutes later the tall man came back into the room where I was and again gestured for me to follow him. Once again, I stood up and followed without hesitation. We went to the same room down the hall where I was asked to sit on the bed once again. Again, he left the room, and again I was able to retrieve my senses and left the room—this time not returning to the other room but leaving the building altogether to maintain my autonomy. I had an uncanny sense that I had met the devil. I was very apprehensive about this experience – this feeling of being unable to control my own thoughts and behavior when in this person's presence,

It is like Harker's experience with Dracula. Whenever the Count is present, Harker feels under his spell, but when the Count is absent during the day, Harker's ego strength rebounds, giving him a chance to reassert some self-control, providing him with the conscious ability to assess the situation and to fight back.

In Jungian theory Harker's ability to reassert some self-control is the equivalent of bringing consciousness to a "complex" and thereby reducing its overall influence and power. Without consciousness, Harker will likely just blindly follow Dracula's commands, like a sheep going to the slaughter. And like the experienced film flam artist, this is exactly what Dracula (and the psychopath) intend and hope for.

This decreasing consciousness is once again exemplified later in the story when Renfield states to Dr. Seward: "I don't want to talk to you: you don't count now; the Master is at hand." (112) Prior to this exchange, Renfield and Seward had had many significant interactions. Seward is the chief psychiatrist at the asylum, and Renfield is one of his more fascinating patients. Seward was attempting to treat Renfield's mysterious affliction. However, as the Master draws nearer, Seward's influence over Renfield begins to decrease proportionately.

The above process parallels the Lonnie Athens Model mentioned earlier. The process takes time. It proceeds step by step. One doesn't just become dark-adapted overnight nor does one become light adapted over-day. Upon reflection, Renfield's relationship with Dracula represents the quintessential example of an identification with the aggressor. Renfield aligns himself with the most powerful figure in this drama to place himself in what he believes will be the least vulnerable position going forward.

Dr. Seward writes about the same phenomenon, this dark and yet unknown influence, when he records the following in his diary about his observations of Lucy, the first English victim of the vampire's bite. He writes:

> It struck me as curious that the moment she became conscious she pressed the garlic flowers close to her. It was certainly odd that whenever she got into that lethargic state, with the stertorous breathing, she put the flowers from her; but that when she waked she clutched them close. There was no possibility of making any mistake about this, for in the long hours that followed, she had many spells of sleeping and waking and repeated both actions many times. (173)

The garlic flowers are placed there by Dr. van Helsing because they represent a deterrent, or obstacle, to reduce the power of the vampire. Thus, the flowers are a subtle aid and stimulant to Lucy's consciousness in her struggle for her self-preservation. Whenever Lucy's consciousness asserts its defenses, the flowers are drawn near. Whenever the vampire complex grabs the upper hand by obfuscating her ability to attend, the flowers are pushed away.

Unfortunately for Lucy, Dracula finds a way to thwart all these attempts to stifle his control. He transforms Lucy into a vampire through the mechanism of Dark Adaptation. This occurs through the (symbolic) blending of the vampire's blood with the blood of Lucy, the human host. The heroic efforts to keep Lucy alive are unsuccessful, despite four transfusions of blood into her depleted body. Her defenders, you see, are only now becoming aware and conscious themselves of their adversary's strengths and overall purpose. And as they learn about their foe certain advantages that favor their objective, his destruction, begin to accumulate. For example, their tendency to be hoodwinked by Dracula is decreased as their facility to spot and defend themselves against Dracula increases. This represents the fruits of their growing consciousness.

Another aspect of Dracula's powers is his ability to affect people from a distance. He demonstrates the skill to exert psychological control over both Renfield and Lucy long before he arrives in England. Both seem to unconsciously respond to his influence (as an individual might be moved by an unseen archetypal energy) and are slowly drawn into his hypnotic web. Since there is at first no direct linear connection between Dracula and these individuals, this writer intuits that there must be an aspect of "synchronicity" at work here. Jung's acausal principle provides the story with a means for unconnected events to be connected in a meaningful way.

Hopcke states:

> Synchronicity is a principle that links events acausally, that is, in terms of the subjective meaningfulness of the coincidence, rather than by cause and effect. Thus, understanding synchronicity and synchronistic events requires a way of thinking almost entirely foreign to Western culture, a way of thinking that does not separate the physical world from interior psychic events. The phrase that often occurs about Jung's concept of synchronicity is unus mundus, Latin for "one world." Synchronicity requires that one consider the world a unified field in which subject and object are fundamentally one, two different manifestations of the same basic reality. (72)

Thus, it seems as though the characters in Stoker's story are placed upon a giant spider web and Dracula, the spider, manages the vibrations from afar and manipulates this transpersonal space to his advantage. He is aware of others long before they are aware of him —an advantage that the vampire or psychopath has over others. They are usually aware of you long before you are aware of them.

When I worked in the prison an observed piece of wisdom was the fact that inmates can think about their captors 24 hours times seven and make deductions that can help them in their attempts to manipulate the system. This advanced awareness might involve the ability to make use of telepathic communications. Schwartz, in Chapter Five of Storm's (2008) *Synchronicity:*

Multiple Perspectives on Meaningful Coincidence, states that "Synchronicity, in addition to having a causal vertical connection between happenings and a horizontal connection between events, might also involve telepathy." (67) And the use of telepathy can be a powerful tool in a vampire's (or psychopath's) arsenal.

Being able to comprehend and control the horizontal and the vertical, as well as the diagonal lines of communication and perception, keeping in mind Jung's transference diagram in the *Practice of Psychotherapy* (CW 16, ¶422), allows one to access the various intra—and inter -psychological paths of unconscious and conscious communications, which then can be used for either good or for bad purposes. (See Fig. 2, next page.) Like a seasoned chess or poker player, the wise analyst, or an observant detective, the criminal mind can make use of its intuition or keen observations of the physical and emotional behavior of others to detect the vulnerabilities and needs of the individual that they are facing off against. What goes around comes around.

Since Dracula isn't the only one with the ability to read the interpersonal horizontal, vertical, and the diagonal relational sphere, the contest is becoming more even. After he has initiated Mina into the process of becoming a vampire by mingling his blood with hers, she, to Dracula's great undoing, is now able to detect his whereabouts and to access his thoughts as well, which have been heretofore largely hidden.

The telepathic process works both ways and, in her musings, Mina comes to this realization through an intuition. She asks van Helsing to hypnotize her while it is still dark, as she knows that the vampire will still be active prior to his returning to his coffin during the daylight hours. Mina has sensed that a part of her has resonated with Dracula for some time, and she wants to exploit

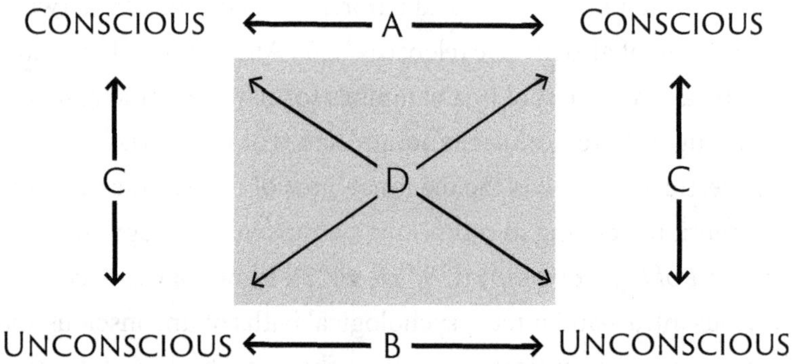

CONSCIOUS ←——— A ———→ CONSCIOUS

C

D

C

UNCONSCIOUS ←——— B ———→ UNCONSCIOUS

A to A. One person relating consciously to another person and vice versa.

B to B. One person relating unconsciously to another person and vice versa.

C to C. One person's unconscious / conscious intra-relationship.

D to D. One person's unconscious / conscious relationship with another person.

Keep in mind that the top line A represents the part of ourselves that is most conscious and regulated by the ego. It is, however, like the tip of a psychological iceberg. So much that influences our behavior is unconscious, occluded, felt- but not seen, and perhaps hiding under our nose. The astute observer has a chance, however, to notice what the otherwise distracted or unobservant individual either misses or fails to intuit.

Fig. 2. My take on Jung's Diagram of the Transference

this connection. The great battle between the humans and the demon has become increasingly more of an even fight.

Dracula begins to display a trait, however, that we learned about from the Athen's model, namely 'Violent Subjugation.' Dracula, a supreme narcissist and tyrant, is not someone who allows disobedience. He is easily irritated and then enraged at the first sign of any challenge to his authority. He had no hesitancy to violently put down even the most modest or compelling of protests.

We see this type of response in many of the authoritarian regimes around the world whose leaders will not tolerate the smallest protest. An example of Dracula's cruelty and irritation at being challenged manifested early in the novel when Harker was still a captive in the castle. He witnesses the importuning mother accosting Dracula in the courtyard of his castle. She is asking for her child to be returned to her.

Dracula has made it a habit to steal the young in the surrounding area of his castle because they make an easy prey. Their young blood also serves to sustain Dracula as well as the other vampires in the castle. The mother (Stoker, 1897/2005) whose child had been taken comes to the castle distraught over the disappearance of her baby and shouts: "Monster, give me my child." (51) But does Dracula show pity? Is he moved by some human sentimentality? No! He is angry that anyone would question or try to interfere with his behavior. Harker describes what happens next:

Somewhere high above, probably on the tower, I heard the voice of the Count calling in a harsh, metallic whisper. His call seemed to be answered from far and wide by the howling of wolves. Before many minutes had passed a pack of them poured, like a pent-up dam when liberated, through the wide entrance into the courtyard. There was no cry from the woman, and the howling of the wolves was but short. Before long they streamed away singly, licking their lips. I could not pity her, for I knew what had become of her child, and she was better dead. (52)

Later in the story, when Renfield has been stirred by Mina's kindness, a kindness that modulates his Dark Adaptation ever so slightly, he confesses to van Helsing and to the others that Mina is at risk. This is an example of how love and kindness can turn someone toward righteousness if they have not already been lost.

Dracula, however, unbeknownst to the others, has already begun to suck the life out of Mina. No one has suspected this since Mina had been sequestered and presumed to be out of harm's way. Dracula, of course, has sensed an opening and exploited this naïveté. Most psychopaths have this uncanny ability to exploit the weaknesses and vulnerabilities of unsuspecting innocents around them, and Dracula is a master at exploitation.

Meanwhile, when Dracula discovers that Renfield has betrayed him, he kills Renfield by smashing his head against the floor and breaking his back. This punishment is unmeasured and excessive, but it ensures that Renfield will never cross the Count again. A short time later when Dracula is with Mina alone, he expresses his contempt for her and the others in their attempt to outwit and defeat him. Dracula states:

And so, you, like the others, would play your brains against mine. You would help these men to hunt me and frustrate me in my designs! You know now, and they know it in part already, and will know in full before long, what it is to cross my path. They should have kept their energies for use closer to home. Whilst they played wits against me—against me who commanded nations, and intrigued for them, and fought for them, hundreds of years before they were born—I was countermining them. And you, their best beloved one, are now to me, flesh of my flesh; blood of my blood; kin of my kin; my bountiful wine press for a while; and shall be later on my companion and my helper. You shall be avenged in turn; for not one of them but shall minister to your needs. But as yet you are to be punished for what you have done. You have aided in thwarting me; now you shall come to my call. When my brain says, "Come!" to you, you shall cross land or sea to do my bidding; and that ends this! (314)

In attempting to establish rapport with such a dark-adapted individual, especially a psychopath, there is no light at the end of the therapy tunnel, only additional darkness. Structure and the team approach are crucial, and no one should ever try to match wits with such an individual on their own. It is a fool's errand.

If there seems to be any light at all, it is likely the light of misplaced optimism, something that the therapist must learn to readily recognize. Most research studies have concluded that there are no positive treatment effects for individuals who are psychopaths (Hare, 1970; Meloy, 2000) and some research has even suggested that treatment only creates better psychopaths (Rice,1992). According to Robert Hare,

Most therapy programs do little more than provide psychopaths with new excuses and rationalizations for their behavior and new insights into human vulnerability They may learn new and better ways of manipulating other people, but they make little effort to change their own views and attitudes or to understand that other people have needs, feelings, and rights. Actually, they see no reason to change. (1993, 196-197)

Despite Dracula's lack of empathy and his apparent cold-bloodiness Mina Harker manages to understand that Dracula also suffers from some terrible affliction, one that she would not want to wish upon anyone. Although she has as much reason to hate this diabolical demon as anyone, she is able to recognize that Dracula also needs forgiveness and understanding, even if Dracula himself is oblivious to this need. For how else are these individuals to heal, either in this generation or in this next so that their plight dies with them and does not continue to contaminate the next generation? There must be some capacity within humankind to both love and forgive at the deepest levels of our hearts, even the most hideous of actions. Mina states:

Jonathan dear, and you all my true, true friends, I want to bear something in mind through all this dreadful time. I know that you must fight—that you must destroy even as you destroyed the false Lucy so that the true Lucy might live hereafter; but it is not a work of hate. The poor soul who has wrought all this misery is the saddest case of all. Just think what his joy will be when he, too, is destroyed in his worser part that his better part may have spiritual immortality. You must be pitiful to him, too, though it may not hold your hands from his destruction. (336)

Before concluding this chapter, I would like to address the incident in Stoker's book when Dracula saves Harker from the three female vampires who are about to feast on his healthy blood. In this scene Harker has been exploring the castle and becomes sleepy. He is tempted, with a lapse in judgment, to rest where he is. However, the Count has forewarned him that to fall asleep in any area other than his designated quarters is to invite "...bad dreams for those who sleep unwisely. Be warned." (38) Harker ignores this advice. His curiosity gets the best of him. He is lulled into a reduced level of consciousness (an *abaissement du niveau mental*) and is thus exposed to the danger that he might, if more conscious, have otherwise avoided, or perhaps proceeded more carefully.

The three female vampires observe his complacency, however, and begin to set upon him with the purpose of sucking his blood. Dracula, however, intervenes and harshly reminds the three subservient vampires that Harker belongs to him. One of the female vampires is taken aback by Dracula's strong attachment and states: "You yourself never loved; you never love." (45) The Count, after looking at Harker attentively, states in a soft whisper: "Yes, I too can love; you yourselves can tell it from the past. Is it not so?" (45)

These individuals are all anima figures who have touched Dracula in some meaningful way. In the process of sucking their blood and changing them into full-fledged vampires Dracula had to first interact with them and with all their human qualities and desires. In these moments he subjected himself to the unconscious pull of the archetypal Self and its command to become whole. But his affiliation to the dark was too strong and this fascination with human attachment did not hold.

This dynamic with the female vampires, in Jungian terms, is what we would call a "lesser *coniunctio*." It will not hold Dracula's attention in a sustainable way —the way that Mina's purity, the main ingredient is establishing a lasting, greater *coniunctio* will, later in the story.

When you take this scenario and you combine it to the account of the Count's death: "... there was a look of peace, such as I never could have imagined might have rested there," (408) you get the strong impression that the Count has in some major way been tormented by his own condition and that, all things being equal, he would have much preferred to be a normal human being suffering the usual slings and arrows of life if only he would have been rescued earlier in his existence by unconditional love.

I mention the two scenes above, the account of Dracula and the other vampires and the issue of love, the greater *coniunc-tio*, and the vampire's death to underscore the potential that the vampire and the psychopath, given the right circumstances can grow toward the light.

In Werner Herzog's 1979 movie *Nosferatu*, for instance, Dracula is destroyed at the end of the story when he becomes enamored with Lucy. She, in trying to find a way to destroy Dracula, becomes aware that "the love of a pure hearted woman can distract the vampire" and cause him to stay too long and be exposed to the light. This will then bar his return into darkness and result in his demise, thus assuring his transformation and redemption.

Something about the experience of love is seductive to the vampire as it is to all of us, but pure love is what can be transformative even to the darkest adapted among us. Perhaps it is simply a matter that "opposites" attract, and they do so because each has something essential to offer the other in terms of wholeness.

Love, it seems, can denude the vampire of all his dark inclinations, or at least it is the best way to attenuate their overall dark grip on the vampire's motivation and focus. Thus, love is the anecdote to isolation and hate. It can melt and dissolve that which has prevented empathic association with others. That is, if it can get past the well-constructed barriers to its felt presence.

I am, however, skeptical that pure love can change a psychopath. If Dracula represents an aspect of a person but not the primary identity, then yes, perhaps it is possible. But the fantasy of being a Mina is how so many women get caught in relationships with dark-adapted individuals: they hope that their love will be transformative.

In contrast to vampires and psychopaths, "antisocial individuals in our correctional and forensic treatment facilities have tended to demonstrate some modest positive treatment effects." (Meloy, 1995) As a result, it is of the utmost importance, especially with limited funds, to differentiate antisocial individuals from vampires (pure psychopaths) when deciding which individuals will benefits from treatment. Montague Summers (1991) defines a vampire in the following way:

> It has been said that a saint is a person who always chooses the better of the two courses open to him at every step. And so, the man who is truly wicked is he who deliberately always chooses the worse of the two courses. Even when he does things, which could be considered right, he always does them for some bad reason. To identify oneself in this way with any

given course requires intense concentration and iron strength of will, and such persons become vampires. (78)

Summer's definition of a vampire comes as close to defining what an evil person might be as any I have encountered. His emphasis on the fact that it takes an "intense concentration and iron will" to qualify further convinces me that such individuals are outliers several standard deviations away from the norm.

That said, we should always remember what Mina has stated, that is, that the monster (psychopath) may be the "saddest case of all." But Mina also stated, with a stern conviction, that this empathy toward the vampire must not stay your hand in his destruction but will allow your resolve to be based in love.

CHAPTER 7

THE PHANTOM OF THE OPERA

Hate, Power, Love, and Redemption

PCL-R score= 16 (Very mild range)

"AN OPERA IS AN extended dramatic work in which the parts are sung to orchestral accompaniment." (*Webster's Dictionary*, 1998). Its themes are the archetypal stuffing that fill life to its greatest capacity. These themes include love, hate, betrayal, jealousy, faith, tenacity, good, evil, triumph, defeat, the masculine and feminine —all contributing to a spectacle that finds a way to reach each person in the audience with affective resonance.

What better place to tell the story of a character who lurks on the periphery of human existence, one who has been barred from the Garden of Eden, not by an Archangel, but by his fellow man. The Phantom, because of this exclusion, and not unlike Dr. Frankenstein's Creature, sets out to strategically extract revenge for the slights and insults that he has endured at the hands of his mother and the larger collective. Like a law of physics, an offense that has been committed always requires a balancing response of equal proportions to be resolved.

HATE

Before delving into the story of the Phantom let me first share a few preliminary thoughts about the author, Gaston Leroux. The characters in a novel, as the reader will know, will oftentimes divulge things about its writer just as all psychological theories are, in some way, a snapshot into the individual personality that theorizes.

According to Katherine Wiswell, in her introduction to the Easton Press 2006 edition of *The Phantom of the Opera*, Leroux wanted nothing more his whole life than to become a writer. His wealthy father, however, appears to have had "higher ambitions" for his only son. In pursing these ambitions, he would make the same mistake that many parents make when envisioning and planning the future of their offspring. He would forget that the primary job of a parent is to assist their child to become an authentic, whole self, not simply a human puppet that fulfills some unresolved need or longing of a parent. But as the age-old adage goes: The sins of the father can often be passed onto the son.

Leroux, evidently, loved to read Dumas and Hugo and his true passion for writing took as its main motif, the story of the hero. Perhaps this was Leroux's unconscious way to overcome or attenuate the power of his father, if only at first, through imagination and fanciful undertakings. His father, steeped in practicality and with a sense of the world, wanted Gaston to study law. He used his patriarchal powers to both shape and direct his son's activities.

Fortunately, like Jung and his father, Leroux's father 'died in time' and the young Leroux was set free from his father's authority to pursue his career as a writer. It turns out, however, that it was not to be that simple. Leroux had to first face several unforeseen additional psychological hurdles within himself. For even in death his father continued to haunt Leroux from the grave, though not in a way that one might expect.

The father had indeed left Leroux a hefty inheritance, but instead of providing Leroux with the freedom to write, it provided him with an amnesty from discipline and the means to avoid writing.

The death of his father apparently unshackled a heretofore thwarted internal desire to rebel against the parental authority, only this time Leroux rebeled unwittingly against his own authority. He quickly squandered his inherited money on wine, women, gambling, and song and is subsequently left without any resources. He hit the proverbial 'rock bottom.'

Yet, just as the ego of the potential hero arrives at the point of defeat, the archetypal Self, the archetype that promotes wholeness and integration, can, in this moment of struggle, provide the spark, or the inspiration, to go on. A new door can open that wasn't previously noticed. A path can appear in what had once been a dead end. And with these unforeseen, hopeful developments, Leroux seizes his chance to re-discover his authentic voice.

POWER

To shed light on the complex nature of *The Phantom of the Opera* (Leroux, 2006) I would like to start my analysis of the Phantom with the Persian's narrative, which provides several insights into the formation of Erik's character. According to the Persian, Erik "is also, in certain respects, a regular child, vain and self-conceited, and there is nothing he loves so much, after astonishing people, as to prove all the really miraculous ingenuity of his mind." (270)

This description of Erik, in and of itself, is nothing unusual. Every child has a desire to shine and to receive praise. Every child, and every person for that matter, wants to celebrate his or her own value and uniqueness. This need, however, will be, to some extent, effected either positively or negatively by the limits set by the expectations of the collective culture. The best-case scenario involves striking a balance between the exertions of the child and the external limits placed upon them. Jung himself was always reminding us that individuation must serve the collective as well as the individual. Jung states:

Individualism means deliberately stressing and giving prominence to some supposed peculiarity rather than to the collective considerations and obligations. But individuation means precisely the better and more complete fulfillment of the collective qualities of the human being, since adequate consideration of the peculiarity of the individual is more conducive to a better social performance than when the peculiarity is neglected or suppressed. The idiosyncrasy of the individual is not to be understood as any strangeness in his substance or in his components, but rather as a unique combination, or gradual differentiation, of functions and faculties, which in themselves are universal .(CW7, ¶267)

Erik's life, almost from the start, demonstrates a defensive element of grandiosity. He is unable to tolerate the multiple external frustrations of his hopes, wants, and desires, and must create, within himself, a fantasy world that supplies what is missing. Grandiosity is an inflation and defense against the shame and sense of having no value. There is simply nothing present in his social surround, at least initially, to keep him attached to his family or others who may be nearby. He must look elsewhere to find these missing elements.

To accomplish this, Erik leaves France and travels to the orient where he serves and ingratiates himself with an autocratic ruler and learns the fine art of torture while concomitantly perfecting his innate abilities as musician and singer. These developments allow for a limited relationship with others by providing him with a working persona, but they do not go far enough to promote a capacity for true intimacy, trust, and love. All these things remain as unconscious, open wounds, covered up for now, and in need of healing.

It is here that we learn about the background and history of this intriguing individual, one whom Katherine Wiswell (2006) described as a "cleaver blending of the classic fairy tale *Beauty and the Beast* and the much darker Faustian legend." (xiii) Wiswell states,

> The Phantom deals with the classic tale of a beautiful soul entrapped in a hideous body that strikes fear and disgust in the hearts of every onlooker. Erick was born disfigured, so he was never appreciated for his brilliant mind and eerily beautiful music. He is literally the classic Beast, ultimately set free by the love of a beautiful young woman. (xiii-xiv)

But how does "love" come to play such a role? If the beautiful soul is trapped within an ugly body how does love assist it to become un-trapped? In the story of *Beauty and the Beast* (Zipes/ de Beaumont, 1989), we see such a scenario and how it plays out. And it is noteworthy, that after Beauty declares her love for Beast, and his more bestial aspects begin slowly to dissolve, transforming him again into a handsome prince, that Beauty is unable to forget Beast. She has fallen in love with Beast—not the current prince. She has fallen in love with the essence of Beast, and this includes all his shortcomings and blemishes. And out of longing for these now missing parts Beauty asks the Prince, what has happened to Beast?

The Prince replies:

> You are looking at him right at your feet. A wicked fairy condemned me to remain in this form until a beautiful girl consented to marry me, and she prohibited me from revealing my intelligence. You were the only person in the world kind enough to allow the goodness of my character to touch you.(146)

In the stories of *Beauty and the Beast*, and *The Phantom of the Opera*, with their themes of ugliness and beauty, we are again reminded of the Creature in Shelly's (1816) Frankenstein. We have a heart that is willing to love but an outward ugliness that interferes with every chance for someone to see the beauty that lies just below the surface. Several clichés immediately come to mind: "Beauty is only skin deep." "Don't judge a book by its cover." "She's not pretty but she has a nice personality." All such statements try to convince the reader that there is more to a situation than meets the eye. But as we are all aware, many people either do not look below the surface or lack the curiosity or energy to do so. Like Cain, a character's unique unresolved flaw will continue unabated. It will interfere with the connections to a larger life. And instead of resolution, such scenarios can promote an alternative path that leads to Dark Adaptation. Why, after all, is the Prince turned into a beast? Is this action by a "wicked fairy" an aspect of the unconscious' aim to balance out, over the course of the story, a persona-bound ego? Is it simply inevitable?

Upbringing

When Erik, as a child, needs love and caring, he is relegated to the back room or to the bowels of the Paris Opera House. He is not given a seat at the family table. He is, in essence, being conditioned to live life on the fringes of society as an outcast. Like Dracula, there is no reflection of a true self in the mirror. Nothing, in his childhood, is mirrored back to him from others that in any way signifies to him his authentic value as a person. He experiences only the sense that he is not wanted, that he is something that others wish to discard. There is no one interested in his identity or in his potential gifts.

The Mask

Instead of developing a healthy sense of his true self, Erik, as a young toddler, is given a mask by his mother to wear to cover his ugly face. He is given, in essence, a false persona to inhabit that, in turn, will not subject others to any personal discomfort. His true self is pushed into the recesses of the unconscious. Parts of himself are forced to be hidden away. This mask will also shield others from a responsibility to own their own shortcomings which they can readily project onto Erik. The insufficiency of parental love in the light of a "special needs child" will oftentimes get overlooked. These children are simply labeled difficult and problematic.

As I have indicated in an earlier part of this book, the collective is often quick to condemn and slow to understand. If we could just stay long enough to hear the true music of another's soul, wouldn't it make all the difference? Instead, it is just easier to turn away, especially when the music is atonal.

Also, parents may sense that they will be judged negatively for having produced such a child. Perhaps they have already rendered such a judgment about themselves. Perhaps they have attempted to shield themselves from such judgment. Erik, after all, is a creation of their union, a creation that both parents now want to distance themselves from like Frankenstein and his creation. Erick has become, in so many words, the receptacle into which his parents and others readily projected their own shadowy, castoff aspects.

He represents the scapegoat that immunizes the "we" of the collective from our darker selves. In terms of object relations theory, Erik becomes the receptacle of negative projections that begin to populate his inner psychological world.

This, in my opinion, reinforces a tendency toward Dark Adaptation. Erik finds comfort in the dark and by seeking an existence on the periphery of society. This Dark Adaptation, however, misunderstood by the values and rules of the majority, provides Erik with his sense of identity. It endows him with purpose and a place, two ingredients that all human beings need. He finds joy in enumerable and creative ways to make others suffer. And while this makes him feel powerful it also allows him inadvertently to see and to feel a connection to the others who have suffered at his hands. So, while Erik's creativity is fueled by a conscious 'hate' it is also nourished by an unconscious need to connect to others in a more positive way. This connection with others is what will make him more fully human.

THE FIRST SPARK

Erik, as he conceives himself to be, can manufacture additional masks to make forays into the world only under the cover of intrigue, darkness, deceit, and shadow. He does not lose all inclination toward the light, however. A part of him, tucked away like Frankenstein's Creature, still longs for a genuine interstitial connection with others though he is very cautious regarding any type of human connection. This caution sometimes causes him to miss these opportunities altogether.

In one salient encounter, however, when Erik is sentenced to be executed during his time in the far east, he is able to escape his fate due to the assistance of an individual called the Persian. Erik discovers through the Persian's kindness that his life is not totally devoid of people who demonstrate caring. This simple life-saving act by the Persian will prove to be decisive to the story's outcome.

RETURN TO PARIS

After Erik's return to Paris following his long adventure to the orient, his need for human connection is further awakened by something which draws him up and out of the bowels of the Paris Opera House. In the basement of this magnificent structure Erik has created a secret abode on its lowest level. The Opera House is a place that he knows very well because his father was the architect. During construction Erik was often given free rein to explore the site and he knows all the nooks and crannies like the back of his hand. From this hidden abode, he can secretly visit the world and extract his revenge on others without being detected. He does so with great success.

But during these vengeful escapades something else catches Erik's attention that begins to draw him up to the higher levels of the opera house for reasons that have nothing to do with revenge. It is the voice of the beautiful Christine Daae, an understudy to the Diva Carlotta, which he hears one evening. He is drawn to her voice like a bee towards honey.

And Erik, an ever-keen observer of others, immediately remembers that he once heard Christine's father talking to her about the Angel of Music. As children Erik and Christine's families had lived near each other, and Erik and Christine had often played together. In his astute manner Erik has always taken the measure of each person he has encountered. He could use this information to later fortify his physical and psychological defenses when negotiating whatever situations might arise.

In Christine's case, however, something different is happening. Instead of bolstering his defenses Erik decides to do something quite out of character. He believes that he has finally found a way to reach out to another heart. While this inclination appears to manifest out of thin air, in truth, it had been lying in wait for this opportunity to exert itself. This is the very potential that was first birthed by the Persian's kind act. Erik now recalls that Christine's father once promised her that the Angel of Music would visit her at some point, as he visits all great musicians. This angel would help her to become an inspired singer. Erik utilizes his memory of the Angel of Music to surreptitiously engage Christine.

Erik intuits this emotional opening, and he comes to Christine in her hour of need. Christine has been apparently overshadowed by many less talented individuals who just happen to have more inflated self-confidence. Christine is in a vulnerable spot and has lost her way without the loving guidance of her deceased father. Her mother has also been dead a long time. And so, Erik makes use of Christine's vulnerability and underlying longing to create a path to her heart. She has been waiting for this Angel of Music to appear and Erik has found a way for the angel to make his appearance. When the angel mysteriously appears, there is a natural openness to the angel's offerings. In this role as the angel, Erik finds that he can authentically, simply be himself. His musical gifts are after all genuine and advanced and his behavior is heartfelt.

In reaching out Erik further discovers an empathy for Christine's predicament, an empathy which begins to feed his own soul. He recognizes that Christine has also been disallowed a place on the bigger stage of life, and he sees them as two sides of the same coin. He also believes that she has the capacity to surely understand and appreciate his own struggles. Erik uses his great skill as a singer to help Christine to develop her heretofore suppressed talent into something truly sublime.

As his efforts succeed Erik increasingly fantasizes that Christine will naturally look beyond his outward appearance and fall in love with him. Her love, in turn, will save him from a continuous, self-imposed, life of isolation. Christine has responded to his offerings and is drawn to and appreciative of his gifts. She is not content, however, to simply follow his instructions and to play by his structured rules. She wants to know who this angel is in the flesh.

Erik, who to this point has been very careful not to show himself, masked or unmasked, only exacerbates Christine's curiosity about the angel. Recall Semele's desire to see Zeus in all his glory, or the many wives of Bluebeard who find they must explore the room that is off limits. It is just such interest that moves

The Phantom

stories along. Although interest can result in a deeper connection, curiosity can also kill the cat. It is not a surprise, however, that Christine, as well as the Persian, have made the strongest connection with the authentic Erik. The Persian had saved Erik's life. Now Christine is on the verge of possibly saving his soul.

BEING HELD CAPTIVE

Erik is afraid to show his face to Christine. After they meet in person, he becomes desperate and overwhelmed with anxiety over his mounting fears of Christine's possible rejection. He takes Christine captive and takes her down to his underworld abode in the opera house. She is immediately missed and her fiancé and others commence to search for her.

Christine, now held against her will, and frightened by Erik's erratic behavior, somehow remains intrigued by this sublime individual who wears a mask. She experiences an increasing compulsion to pull the mask from Erik's face. She is not simply lulled into acquiescence because of his multitude of talents, nor is she cowered by his apparent cruelty and thirst for power. Instead, Christine finds herself involved in a mystery and feels compelled to push past the many seemingly impossible obstacles. She is pulled, some would say without choice, into finding out who Erik is at the center of his being. And this is exactly the kind of person that the Phantom has needed if he is to grow beyond his entrenched disposition.

Christine described her behavior as she removed the mask: "Suddenly, I felt a need to see beneath the mask. I wanted to know the face of the voice, and with a movement, which I was utterly, unable to control; swiftly my fingers tore away the mask. Oh, horror, horror, horror." (170)

Erik responded:

Know that I am built up of death from head to foot and that it is a corpse that loves you and adores you and will never, never leave you! Look, I am not laughing now, I am crying, crying for you, Christine, who have torn off my mask, and who therefore can never leave me again! As long as you thought me handsome, you could have come back, but now that you know my hideousness, you would run away for good... So, I shall keep you here! Why did you want to see me! When my own father never saw me and when my mother, so as to not see me, made me a present of my first mask! (173)

Then Christine continues, after some reflecting on Erik's face:

He had let go of me at last and was dragging himself about on the floor, uttering terrible sobs. And then he crawled away like a snake, went into his room, closed the door, and left me alone to my reflections. Presently I heard the sound of the organ; and then I began to understand Erik's contemptuous phrase when he spoke about opera music. What I heard now was utterly different from what I had heard up until then. His Don Juan Triumphant (for I had not a doubt that he had rushed to his masterpiece to forget the horror of the moment) seemed to me at first one long, awful, magnificent sob. But, little by little, it expressed every emotion, every suffering of which mankind is capable. It intoxicated me; and I opened the door that separated us. Erik rose, as I entered, but dared not turn in my direction. Erik, I cried, show me your face without fear. I swear that you are the most unhappy and sublime of men; and, if ever again I shiver when I look at you, it will be because I am thinking of the splendor of your genius. Then Erik turned around, for he believed me, and I also had faith in myself. He fell at my feet, with words of love... with words of love in his dead mouth... and the music had ceased... he kissed the hem of my dress and did not see that I had closed my eyes. (173-174)

Erik is most likely not even aware of this 'part of himself' until the person of Christine begins to work her magic. She is the necessary catalyst, like the analyst is for the analysand. For to be denied love is untenable in the long run. It is indeed unjust. It can become the fertile ground that finds its voice through the manipulation and control of others.

But to be cast into the loneliness of the dark (as with Lucifer being cast into the fiery pit) is insufficient in itself to dull the longing for human connection. Even Lucifer who states (Milton) "it is better to rule in hell than to serve in heaven" (Book One, 9) must find a way to mess with God and his creation. He is not simply content with staying in the dark. Something compels him to explore the regions of light as we see depicted with Shelly's Creature and with Nosferatu's infatuation with Lucy in the (1979) film directed by Werner Herzog. We Jungians might say that such an infatuation is the quest for wholeness.

Love

In the French Fairy tale Beauty and the Beast the Prince has been turned into a Beast because he has been insensitive to the love of another. Like Narcissus who ignores Echo and is punished by Nemesis (Cotterell and Storm, 2003, 65), the Prince has hurt someone who loves him and is punished for his insensitivity. He is told that the only way that he can recover his former self is to earn the love of someone despite his beastly looks and ways.

Erik has a similar fate, although we are not given any mythical account to justify it. Despite his ugliness, however, he still longs for relationship. When he reflects upon Christine and her belief in the "Angel of Music," like Frankenstein's Creature and the blind old man in the cottage, he starts to imagine that someone could love him if only they might see past his ugliness and experience his finer qualities.

In a way that is exactly what he himself needed to do—see past his own ugliness to experience the gifts that he has. Christine, not knowing what she is getting into, opens her heart to the Angel of Music who represents the visitation that her father had told her to expect. Thus, her defenses are down and her need to believe is high. The two come together like a hand in a glove, but there is only one glove, while there are two hands. This means that such an arrangement will not settle the entire score. More is yet needed.

Redemption

Despite Christine's exposure to Erik's face, she finds a way to not reject him in total. First, perhaps out of self-preservation, she realizes that she must somehow play along with Erik's intentions. She must buy time. She knows that help may be on the way. In this interim of buying time, however, she is touched by the Phantom's inner beauty, much like the Beast touches Beauty. She balances her behavior and corrals her fear long enough to embrace the bigger picture.

Christine's fiancé in the meantime is somehow able to locate Erik's hidden abode, but Erik catches him and locks him in a torture chamber which can be flooded. Erik plans to drown this young man who has tried to take his captive away. The situation seems dire, and resolution seems a far way off.

But despite all this Christine is moved by the Phantom's suffering and can demonstrates her heartfelt concern and sympathy for his agony. He senses her genuine care and feels genuinely loved, by a love that is pure and unselfish.

TRANSFORMATION

After Erik experiences this authentic acceptance and love from Christine he states to Christine and her fiancé: "You are saved, both of you. And soon I shall take you up to the surface of the earth, to please my wife." (329). His wife refers not to Christine but to his own internal anima whom he has married and now integrated in himself as part of the individuation process. This statement represents the culmination of Erik's transformation from the suffering and vengeful Phantom into the Christ like figure who dies so that others may live.

Erik has recognized that Christine has indeed loved him. She has recognized, like Beauty did with the Beast, that Erik has a heart and that he has within him a goodness that has simply not had the proper outlet. Her recognition of this is the elixir that was needed to bring it into fruition. I am reminded of the character Sydney Carton from Dickens' *A Tale of Two Cities* (1859), who finds a way, after a life of leisure and selfishness, to finally do something worthwhile with his life. He exchanges himself for another person awaiting execution in the dungeons of the Bastille and states "... tis a far far better thing than I have ever done.... Tis a far far better place that I go than I have ever been." Like Faust, Carton realizes that it is never too late to make amends. There is always a way to find redemption if the heart is willing. Erik takes this path because he has experienced the power of Christine's love. Toward the end of the story Erik declares to the Persian:

> I am going to die. Of love... daroga... I am dying... of love... That is how it is... I loved her so... And I love her still... daroga... and I am dying of love for her, I... I tell you... If you knew how beautiful she was... when she let me kiss her... alive.... It was the first... time, daroga, the first... time I ever kissed a woman.... Yes, alive.... I kissed her alive... and she looked as beautiful as if she had been dead (332).

Later Erik states:

> Yes, she was waiting for me, waiting for me erect and alive, a real, living bride... as she hoped to be saved... And, when I came forward, more timid than a little child, she did not run away... no, no... she stayed... she waited for me... I even believe... daroga ... that she put out her forehead... a little... oh, not much... just a little... like a living bride... And... and... I... kissed her!... I!...I!... I!... And she did not die... Oh how good

it is, daroga, my poor, unhappy mother would never... let me kiss her... She used to run away... and throw me my mask!... (334).

Further along, Erik states:

Ah, I am not going to die yet... presently I shall... but let me cry!... Listen daroga... listen to this... While I was at her feet... I heard her say, 'Poor, unhappy Erik!'... And she took my hand!... I had become no more, you know, than a poor dog ready to die for her... I mean it, daroga!... I held in my hand a ring, a plain gold ring which I had given her... which she had lost... and which I had found again... a wedding ring, you know... I slipped it onto her little hand and said, There!... Take it... Take it for you... and him!... It shall be my wedding present... a present from your poor, unhappy Erik... I know you love the boy... don't cry anymore!... She asked me, in a very soft voice, what I meant.... Then I made her understand that, where she was concerned, I was only a poor dog, ready to die for her... but that she could marry the young man when she pleased, because she had cried with me and mingled her tears with mine. (335)

Erik is thereby redeemed. Christine's love has supplied the missing part that allows his soul to find peace. Nothing else was required. Some part of the world's soul has been healed.

Werewolf

CHAPTER 8

THE WEREWOLF

PCL-R score = 12 (Very, very mild range of psychopathy)

He loved as he had never loved before—as he had never deemed it possible to love and in his mad worship of the woman, he believed to be as pure as she was fair, he forgot that the devil hides safest where he is least suspected.

—O'DONNELL, 1996, 202-203

Volition, intention, and all personal differentiations are acquired late and owe their existence to a consciousness that has emancipated itself from mere instinctivity.

—JUNG,1964, CW 10, ¶646

When I get angry I close my eyes and see nothing but white. Then wolf comes out.

—INMATE CONVICTED OF NUMEROUS AGGRAVATED ASSAULTS

A MYTHICAL WEREWOLF IS a person who changes from their human form into a devastating creature at night, during the phases of the full moon. Such an individual takes on the characteristics of a wolf, including its cunning and aggressiveness, and will use these abilities to survive, hunt, and assert power over prey and would be adversaries. The word itself is derived from the Anglo-Saxon words 'wer', which means man and the word *wulf*, which means wolf. (O'Donnell, 1996) The combining of the two produces a wolfman or werewolf. Although I do not believe that a person can morph into a half wolf, half human creature, I do believe that inside all of us is an energy, that if released, can thoroughly swamp our more human characteristics, and cause us to act like a ferocious animal.

One aspect in the werewolf legend that I have pondered is the importance of the full moon in regards the transformation process from human to beast. I have wondered why this change occurs only then and not at other times. During my many years of working at various mental institutions I have often discussed with colleagues whether the full moon affects patients, with the so-called lunacy effect. Are some individuals more prone to violence or mania at this time of the month? Everyone seems to concur that there is a "full moon phenomenon" but there has never been to my knowledge any reputable research to back this up. In fact, the available research tends to negate that there is any such effect at all.

Be that as it may on some realistic plane, it is my theory that the full moon, metaphorically speaking, does illuminate what lies fallow in the dark and can energizes that which might otherwise remain dormant. The full moon, much like a large magnet, can increase its magnetic influence, as it gets brighter, larger, and closer. Like a recessive gene whose time in the spotlight has come, something gets activated. The psychological ducks are all in a row. The constellations are lined up just so. And while not all potentials (or archetypes) get activated in any one life or lifetime Jung states that "It is a psychological fact that an archetype can seize hold of the ego and even compel it to act as it—the archetype—wills." (1990, 66). Jung also states that: "The energy of the archetype communicates itself to the ego only when the latter has been influenced or gripped by the autonomous action of the archetype." (66)

WEREWOLF LORE

Well, much has been written about werewolves, but perhaps the first account of a werewolf appeared in the *Book of Daniel* (Chapter Four, Verses 15-33), where it is written that King Nebuchadnezzar exhibited signs of being a werewolf for a period of four years. The largest amount of material on the werewolf, however, seems to have been collected and documented during the Middle Ages (Steiger, 1999) where 30, 000 individuals, accused of werewolfery, were charged, and burned at the stake in France between 1520 and 1630.

According to Frost (2003) "a werewolf is a man or a woman who, voluntarily or involuntarily, is supernaturally transformed into the shape of a wolf or endowed with all the physical characteristics of that animal—a shaggy covering of fur, glowing eyes, long canine teeth, and razor-sharp claws." (6) Initially, there is apparently no awareness on the part of the affected person during their transformed (dissociated) state. Only after the werewolf has returned to its human form is there a potential through a gradual recognition that he or she is the creature who is committing atrocious and violent acts.

This discovery can lead to remorsefulness and the fear of repeating such acts, such as the lead female werewolf in the 1997 movie, *An American Werewolf in Paris* (directed by Anthony Waller), who attempts to kill herself by jumping from the Eiffel Tower so that she will do no more killing. While she is back in her more conscious human form, her pro-social self, like Dr. Jekyll, she looks desperately for a way to stop her nefarious alter-self. She is rescued however, by a young American man who demonstrates his genuine love for her, which in turn, helps her to break the werewolf curse and regain her complete human form.

But, of course, not all werewolves, or criminals for that matter, experience this remorse that prompts them to fight the effects of the Dark Adaptation process. Again, much depends on whether this dark transformative process was sought out or forced upon the individual. At the time of the transformation, it is important to assess how dark-adapted an individual is at the time that he or she acquires this condition. In some cases, heroic attempts are made to find a solution before the werewolf has solidified its dominance and has a chance to kill again. In other cases, there can be a growing willingness to defer to the wolf, especially in such cases where the ego becomes inflated with and addicted to a certain sense of invincibility —like the power gain via the process of "identification with the aggressor" or during Athens' stage of "Violent Coaching." (1992)

WEREWOLF COMPLEX

I refer to the condition described above as the "Werewolf Complex." This complex involves a major battle between the pro-social human being and the beast within. It is the very same struggle that many everyday individuals encounter in their lives. The major delineated characteristic of the Werewolf Complex, as defined by this writer, is that the individual continues to have a bifurcated desire, to varying degrees. One part of the individual clings to the pro-social fabric while the other part embraces the pull of strong antisocial proclivities. It is as if there are two selves vying for dominion. Like Faust, however, the werewolf has not yet been collected by the curator of the Dark. He or she still retains a chance at redemption. Their soul has not yet totally acclimated to darkness. Faust speaks of such redemption when he realizes that God still retains dominion over the devil. He states:

> Deep night now seems to fall more deeply still,
> Yet inside me there shines a brilliant light.
> What I have thought, I hasten to fulfill:
> The master's word alone has real might.
>
> (Goethe, 1990, 463)

Later the Angels sing to the Devil that his claim on the soul of Faust is no longer valid;

> What is not part of your sphere you may not share.
> What fills you with fear you cannot bear.
> If the attacks succeeds,
> We must do violent deeds.
> Love alone leads loving ones there. (481)

This idea that love is the most important salve to werewolves is not surprising. It may well be the salve to all suffering sentient beings. Love is the thing that can heal the disturbed soul. It figures prominently in the first story of the werewolf that I remember seeing in the movies as a child. The movie, *Curse of the Werewolf* (1961), starring Oliver Reed, begins with the rape of an innocent young woman by an old lusting monarch. A child is conceived during this diabolical act, the mother dies in childbirth, and the child is adopted by his grandparents of humble means. Unfortunately, the stain (a form of original sin) emanating from the perverse conception predisposes the child psychologically toward an "innate darkness."

To make matters worse, a wolf bites the child, and this allows the darkness within him to multiply. The child, during the phase of the full moon, mysteriously begins to sprout hair all over his body. His teeth are enlarged, and his ears become pointed. He begins to act like a wolf every month for a few days. His grandparents are helplessly confronted by this strange phenomenon.

Not knowing what to do, they seek help from the local priest. This priest, who has knowledge of these strange manifestations, instructs the grandparents about what is required. The priest states that the only hope, the only possible solution to rectify this evil foreboding, is love. He states: "You must love the child with your whole heart and pray to God for his blessing."

The priest's recommendations are followed to the letter and produce positive results. The child grows up to be a very handsome and responsible young man, a pillar in his community. Unfortunately, he falls in love with a certain beautiful young woman (perhaps this is his destiny) who happens to be the daughter of a high-born local baron. This baron, for reasons of pride and a sense of hierarchy, rejects the young man as an appropriate suitor for his daughter. This rejection, in turn, resurrects the old werewolf complex, which had been sealed over by the healing powers of love. The wolf complex within is once again animated and set loose. The complex, like all complexes, has been lying patiently in wait for a chance to reassert itself.

As the movie progresses the rejected young man above, in his human form, recognizes that he is the human who is transforming into the werewolf and is causing the death and terror that the town is experiencing. Having a good heart that has not been entirely corrupted by the dark adaptation process, he seeks out the hunter with the silver bullet to end his existence before he can kill again. The goodness in his heart, born out of the love given to him by his grandparents and the woman who loves him, prevents further destruction and tethers him to a path to salvation.

Just today I was discussing a situation with a patient, which in many ways parallels the transformation of a human being into a psychological werewolf. At least it underscores the potential archetypal energy source and illustrates the potential pathway for its emergence. Here is what my patient stated:

I was sitting there having a conversation with my mother. I just couldn't stand what she was talking about. I can't stand what she reads or the shows she watches on television. She was saying that I should just get a job, as though I haven't been trying my best. She wants me to be this intellectual, classy guy. I just feel pushed into accepting a pre-fabricated, boring existence. Then, all of a sudden, I felt this energy coursing through my veins. It was physical. It felt like rage. With no warning, the wooden chair that I was sitting in exploded into pieces. I hadn't done anything to it directly, physically, but it just blew into pieces. Both my mother and I were shocked and couldn't explain what had happened.

The energy in the above vignette exemplifies the power of the complex. Its power demonstrates its ability to swamp an ego that is already taxed to the limit. Thank goodness that in the above situation the chair was the recipient of the rage and not the mother. But given the addition of just a few more proverbial 'pieces of straw' it may well have been the mother. I am working with this patient to help him to understand, contain, and integrate this energy into a larger whole.

This brief clinical example reminded me of the meeting between Jung and Freud in 1909 (Jung, 1963) when they are discussing 'occultism'. In referring to Freud Jung states: "Because of his materialistic prejudice, he rejected this entire complex of questions (about occultism) as nonsensical and did so in terms of so shallow a positivism that I had difficulty in checking the sharp retort on the tip of my tongue." (155) This is when there was a loud crack that came from the bookcase and both Freud and Jung were startled. Jung then states "There, that is an example of the so-called catalytic exteriorization phenomenon." (155) Was this cracking sound coming from the bookcase the result of Jung's projected inner anger? Did this energy need release much like volcanic lava when it bursts out from the side of a mountain that can no longer contain it?

BECOMING A WEREWOLF

If becoming a werewolf resembles to any degree, the same processes involved with the identification with the aggressor process or exposure to "violent coaching" we might also ask ourselves about the short—and long-term effects of military training on certain recruits. For instance, are some individuals more psychologically able to manage their training in the art of killing others?

Without sufficient ego maturity might some individuals become conditioned to like killing, especially if this acquired skill fills a deep void by providing a sense of inflated confidence? Once this inflated power is felt wouldn't there likely be a desire to return to this manic inflation to both maintain the egoistic high and to maintain a sense of self-regulation? I would say yes, that both urges are likely. Killing after all, if not contained can provide an individual with an awesome sense of power. Regardless, it is bound to have an effect that needs care and monitoring from those in charge. My previous analytic supervisor Dr. Hogenson once told me that this is one of the biggest responsibilities of the military command: how to control the killing instinct while keeping the troops well-oiled and disciplined. (Personal Communication).

This tradition of learning how to be a violent warrior has a long history. In Northern Europe there were such groups as the "Berserkers" who trained to bring out the beast from within so that they could frighten and vanquish their enemies. In ancient Sparta young boys were taken from their mothers at age seven to train in military camps where they learned to relinquish sentiment and empathy, two characteristics that would undermine their ability to kill. To care about others and to entertain human feelings toward the enemy has no place on the battlefield. It can take away your edge and get you killed. This concept is brilliantly depicted in Zack Snyder's 2007 movie "300" about the brave men of Sparta who defend Greece against the Persian King Xerces in 350BC at the pass of Thermopile. These Spartans, while fierce and ruthless in battle, were disciplined to an equal degree.

But what happens when the beast doesn't want to return to the barracks. What happens when an individual cannot contain the beast within and is seduced to use such force in places other than the battlefield? Again, if you recall the Athens model, this is what some individuals end up doing. If you look at them the wrong way, they may come after you with a vengeance because their sense of self-esteem has been threatened. Life becomes a battlefield. To such an individual each place and every moment represents a threat that needs to be faced and overcome. An archetypal energy can well up and grab this individual--and woe to the unsuspecting or ill prepared person who happens to be in the path of such an energy!

This causes me to wonder at times about our soldiers who come back from the war after engaging in and experiencing horrible and traumatic events. Many of these same individuals are recruited by police departments around the country, largely because of their toughness and training. But exposure to imminent death in the war zone has a way of firing up the amygdala, and the fight-flight reaction can become entrenched, a major symptom of Post-Traumatic Stress Disorder (PTSD). What is oftentimes attenuated in the folks being recruited as police officers is the capacity to contain anger and to be flexible, even handed, and able to listen to all sides of a story.

Arieti (1967) views the issue of lycanthropy as a process not dissimilar to the Berserkers mentioned above. He likens it to a form of collective psychosis, what Jung refers to as a "participation mystique.." Arieti states:

> The patient assumes the dominant idea of a special group to which he belongs. For instance, like the other members of the group, he believes that he has been transformed into an animal and behaves as that animal would. He may start to bite like a dog or mew like a cat. In other cases, he must imitate the bizarre behavior of the group (dancing in the Saint Vitus dance or convulsing in tarantism or tarantulism. (320)

Similarly, Steiger (1999) states:

> Since earliest times, more levelheaded persons have observed that when a man becomes absolutely filled with rage, he is no longer quite human. One may say that he has given the control of his reason back to the beast within—or one might even say that the enraged man is "beside himself," that he has become something more than himself. Either the beast within or some other supernatural power has now endowed the angered, raging man with more strength and more deadly determination to work harm against his enemy than he had before he became so angry, so berserk. (33)

This being taken over by the beast within is like the transition into a werewolf. According to Steiger,

> When those individuals who became werewolves against their will are not under the power of the curse that forces

them to become ravenous beasts, they experience all the normal human emotions of shame and disgust for the deeds that they must commit under the blood spell. They may long for death and seek ways to destroy themselves before they take the lives of more innocent victims. (17)

Steiger continues:

On the other hand, those who became werewolves of their own choice and who sought power of transmutation through incantations, potions, or spells, glory in their strength and in their ability to strike fear into the hearts of all who hear their piercing howling on the nights of the full moon. (17)

In the two descriptions above, the first group is lighter adapted whereas the second group is more adapted to the dark.

I would like to mention one additional story, Stevenson's (1887) lesser-known work *Olalla*. The story opens with the recovery of a young man from a long war illness. His Doctor states: "... my part is done, and, I may say with some variety, well done. It remains only to get you out of this cold and poisonous city and give you two months of a pure air and easy conscience." (5). To accomplish this the Doctor decides, with input from the local padre, that his patient needs to go to a secluded villa for the final stages of his recovery. The villa is the home of a beautiful young woman, Olalla, who resides there with her brother Felipe and their mother.

At first such arrangements are not possible. The residents of the Villa are a proud family and they apparently do not wish to have anything to do with the outside world, preferring to keep to themselves. There is a reason for their self-imposed seclusion, but that reason is not known at the beginning of the tale. Poverty, however, forces the secluded family to reconsider the padre's request, and the proud family eventually agrees to take in the convalescing soldier. There is one stipulation, however. In the agreement the convalescing soldier must agree to keep to himself and to remain a stranger. The residents wish to keep their distance even from the smallest of intimacies. While this request seems most peculiar, the involved parties agree it to, and the convalescing soldier begin his recuperation in earnest.

The agreement proceeds along smoothly enough until the soldier begins to become curious about the residents of the villa. It is always difficult to ignore where our curiosities lead us! And so, one night the soldier hears a blood-curdling scream and begins to imagine that the daughter, whom he has heard about but not yet seen, is being mistreated in some way. He feels a growing need to probe into this conflict and to interfere if need be.

Like one of Bluebeard's wives, he must investigate what's in the forbidden room. But as he tries to leave his room, he discovers that his door is locked and his urge to investigate the scream is thwarted. His curiosity only grows. And so, we see that the initial boundaries and steps to keep the soldier separate from the inner workings of the family begin to break down. Like an ego that tries to insist on having its way all the time, eventually the unconscious will find a way to break through so that the untold part of the tale can be told. All parts of the whole, you see, have a story to tell, especially those parts that have been sealed up and purposively packed away.

In his daily meanderings the soldier, while exploring different rooms in the building where he resides, happens upon the
following poem left on a writing table:

> Pleasure approached with pain and shame,
> Grief with a wreath of lilies came.
> Pleasure showed the lovely sun.
> Jesu dear, how sweet it shown!
> Grief with her worn hand pointed on,
> Jesu dear, to thee. (38)

The soldier is touched by these words. His previous fear that
someone, perhaps the saintly daughter, is being persecuted in
some way, and must have written these lines, begins to grow
exponentially. He is now drawn to this mysterious woman—
someone whom the padre has emphatically reminded him to
stay away from. She represents however, not simply a person to
be avoided but, I believe, an anima figure in the soldier's psyche
that draws him psychologically toward some challenge that
will help him to grow. The thought of her invites the soldier to
explore heretofore uncharted territory both within and outside of
himself. Perhaps this is the psychological side of his full recovery
from his war wounds.

Anyway, the above poem deals enigmatically with the battle
between dark and light forces, and Jesu is the bearer and the
provider of the light. This family, you see, is a family of werewolves, and they have been given a space to exist, but their ability
to roam about is curtailed by Jesu, who is represented by the
padre who comes to maintain the agreement. This agreement

is put into jeopardy by the presence and the explorations of the soldier.

During one of his daily explorations the soldier finally meets Olalla, and subsequently falls in love with her, and she with him. However, she chooses to forgo this personal love for the soldier to honor a higher commitment. She understands that to give into the love she feels for the soldier will only lead to his destruction. Her devotion to God is what provides her with the strength to shut off the werewolf complex within herself. Olalla, after hearing the soldier's pronouncement of love says in response: "You will go away today." (52)

Of course, the soldier is distraught by Olalla's command to leave and doesn't comply. He becomes more embroiled in the happenings at the Villa, and this leads to his being attacked by the mother in her werewolf state. Olalla and her brother, constrained by their devotion to Jesu, rescue him and finally get him to go away before it is too late. Thus, again we see that an individual werewolf can still exercise restraint, especially while in human form and when operating from a defined structure with a spiritual connection.

CHAPTER 9

DR. JEKYLL AND MR. HYDE

PCL-R Scores: Jekyll = 4 (normal),
Hyde = 33 (highly psychopathic)

AS STATED EARLIER IN this book, Jungians believe, to the benefit of all, that the process of individuation is an undertaking that not only serves the individual but also the collective. This is at the heart of Shakespeare's statement in his play Hamlet spoken by Polonius: "This above all else —to thy own self be true, and it must follow, as night the day, thou canst not be false to any man." (657)

BEGINNINGS

In the fifth gospel of the Christian Bible according to Thomas Jesus notices the frightening sculpted figures, gargoyles, around the doors and windows of Essene churches. (Thoresen, 2018) Out of curiosity, he inquiries about the significance of these figures from one of the Essene priests. He is told that they are there to scare away the evil spirits. Jesus then asks: "Where are these evil spirits scared away to or directed?" (14) Inspired by this exchange I would like to add a few additional questions that could be asked.

Is it proper and right to send evil elsewhere? Is it a righteous act to protect oneself at the expense of some other? Do we, out of convenience, send the evil down the street to our neighbor or to a meeting place of a different faith?

Have you ever heard someone say that there was a plane crash but thank goodness there were no Americans on board? Isn't that like sending what we don't like or accept about ourselves, or the evil that exists within our own community, elsewhere? In my opinion, this happens all the time. It is the ubiquitous attempt to keep separate, good from evil, and light from darkness, and to somehow protect us from ourselves. Remember Pogo's admonishment: "We have met the enemy and he is us." We will see how this foolish strategy plays out in the tragic story of Dr. Jekyll.

DISTINCTLY DIFFERENT VERSUS SUBLIMELY BALANCED

In the beginning of Stevenson's book, *The Strange Case of Dr. Jekyll and Mr. Hyde*, we enter a story that, like life itself, has been going on without us. The reader immediately gets a description of what a healthy balance of psychological opposites might look as described in the long-standing friendship between Mr. Utterson and Mr. Enfield. Utterson is described first:

> ...a man of rugged countenance, that was never lighted by a smile; cold, scanty, and embarrassed in discourse, backward in sentiment; lean, long, dusty, dreary, and yet somewhat lovable. At friendly meetings, and when the wine was to his taste, something eminently human beaconed from his eye; something indeed which never found its way into his talk, but which spoke not only in these silent symbols of an

after-dinner face, but more often and loudly in the acts of his life. He was austere with himself; drank gin when he was alone, to mortify a taste for vintages; and though he enjoyed the theatre, had not crossed the doors of one for twenty years. But he had an approval tolerance for others; sometimes wondering, almost with envy, at the high pressure of spirits involved in their misdeeds, and in any extremity inclined to help rather than to reprove. (3)

Mr. Utterson is also fond of stating: "I incline to Cain's heresy—I let my brother go to the devil in his own way," (3) meaning that he tries not to involve himself in the private affairs of others. Stevenson then informs us: "In this character it was frequently his fortune to be the last reputable acquaintance and the last good influence in the lives of down-going men." (4)

Mr. Enfield, on the other hand, is described as a distant kinsman of Mr. Utterson, and a "well known man about town" (4) He is an extrovert, in contrast, to Mr. Utterson's introversion. He has a bond with Mr. Utterson that others, because of the differences, cannot quite make sense of. Stevenson provides the following sketch of what others observe:

It was reported by those who encountered them in their Sunday walks, that they said nothing, looked singularly bored, and would hail with obvious relief the appearance of a friend. For all that, the two men put the greatest store by these excursions, counted them the chief jewel of each week, and not only set aside occasions of pleasure, but resisted the calls of business, that they might enjoy them uninterrupted. (4)

These two men, while distinctly different—are somehow sublimely balanced in their relationship and well suited for each other's company. Distinctly different might be a way to define opposites while sublimely balanced is a way to describe how opposites, or people of different persuasions can and do learn to appreciate and respect each another. It is also an apt description of a healthy functioning ego that manages the different parts of itself. Keep that idea in the back of your mind as we continue our current, deepening exploration.

During one of their walks Utterson and Enfield happen upon an odd, two-storied structure that "showed no window, nothing but a door on the lower story and a blind forehead of discolored wall on the upper; and bore in every feature the marks of prolonged and sordid negligence." (7) We are alerted by this description to become curious about this prolonged and sordid negligence—for it will likely have symbolic information and value to offer us, as we unpack this story, much like the imagery in a dream.

"Prolonged" and "Sordid Negligence"

Since words are most important to a writer, before we proceed further, let us define these two words, or fingerposts, that Stevenson places in our path. "Prolonged" indicates that something is continuing for a notably long time. "Negligence," on the other hand, suggests an act or instance of being negligent and not taking care of something. In putting these two words together we begin to sense that something has been going on for some time and that this something has not received adequate attention. "Sordid" refers to something dirty, filthy, wretched, or squalid. There is a mystery here asking to be solved—and

"Did you ever remark that door?"

someone, namely Mr. Utterson, seems interested in solving it. These curiosities are the very situations that intrigue us, that rouse our attention, and that cause us to explore life and to uncover new knowledge and previously unknown parts of our wholeness.

As the two gentlemen pass the structure, Mr. Enfield lifts his cane and asks his companion: "Did you ever remark that door?" (7)

When Mr. Utterson replies that he has, Enfield adds—"it is

connected in my mind with a very odd and unusual story." (7-8) Our curiosity has now been peaked and nudged over a threshold which requires further exploration. Curiosity, perhaps our most important instinct, is what causes us to read on.

BACKGROUND OF DR. JEKYLL

Meanwhile, Dr Jekyll, not totally oblivious to his situation, provides us with the following description of what has led up to his current dilemma:

I was born to a large fortune, endowed besides with excellent parts, inclined by nature to industry, fond of the respect of the wise and good among my fellowmen, and thus, as might have been supposed, with every guarantee of an honorable and distinguished future. And indeed, the worst of my faults was a certain impatient gayety of disposition, such as has made the happiness of many, but such as I found it hard to reconcile with my imperious desire to carry my head high and wear a more than commonly grave countenance before the public. Hence it came about that I concealed my pleasures, and that when I reached years of reflection, and began to look round me and take stock of my progress and position in the world, I stood already committed to a profound duplicity of life. Many a man would have even blazoned such irregularities, as I was guilty of; but from the high views that I had set before me, I regarded and hid them with an almost morbid sense of shame. It was thus rather the exacting nature of my aspirations than any degradation in my faults, that made me what I was, and, with even a deeper trench than in most men,

Dr. Jekyll

severed in me those provinces of good and ill which divide
and compound man's dual nature. (97-98)

Jekyll continues,

> Though so profound a double dealer, I was in no sense a hyp-
> ocrite; both sides of me were in dead earnest. I was no more
> myself when I laid aside restraint and plunged in shame, than
> when I labored in the eye of day, at the furtherance of knowl-
> edge or the relief of sorrow and suffering. (98)

OPPOSITES IN HARMONY

I contend that the Utterson and Enfield's relationship, unlike the
description that Jekyll gives above about his "double dealing,"
represents a true acceptance and harmonious blending of opposites, contrasted with Jekyll, who keeps his persona and shadow
sides separate from each other. This blending on the part of the
two friends, positions them, like a healthy functioning ego, to
explore what is behind the aforementioned "prolonged and sordid
negligence." In regards typology, as a team, Utterson and Enfield
are well balanced and suited to venture forth, with curiosity,
into the unfolding story, previously described as "very odd and
unusual."

Now let us return to Mr. Enfield's story about the door. Enfield
states:

> I was coming home from someplace at the end of the world,
> about three o'clock of a black winter morning, and my way
> lay through a part of the town where there is literally nothing

to be seen but lamps. Street after street, and all the folks asleep, street after street, all lighted up as if for a procession and all as empty as a church—till at last I got into that state of mind when a man listens and listens and begins to long for the sight of a policeman. All at once I saw two figures; one a man who was stumping along eastward at a good walk, and the other a girl of maybe eight or ten who was running as hard as she was able down a cross street. Well sir, the two ran into one another naturally enough at the corner; and then came the horrible part of the thing; for the man trampled calmly over the child's body and left her screaming on the ground. It sounds nothing to hear, but it was hellish to see. It wasn't like a man; it was like some damned Juggernaut. I gave a shout, took to my heels, collared the gentleman, and brought him back to where there was already quite a group about the screaming child. He was perfectly cool and made no resistance, but gave me one look, so ugly that it brought out the sweat on me like running. (8)

Mr. Enfield continues his story:

Well, we screwed him up to a hundred pounds for the child's family; he would have clearly liked to stick out; but there was something about the lot of us that meant mischief. The next thing was to get the money; and where do you think he carried us but to that place with the door? He whipped out a key, went in, and presently came back with the matter of ten pounds in gold and a check for the balance on Coutt's, drawn payable to bearer and signed with a name that I can't mention .... (9-10)

Mr. Utterson Outside the Door

After Mr. Utterson learns more about Hyde from Enfield, he sets out to discover additional facts about Hyde, whom Utterson now believes may have some diabolical hold over his friend Dr. Jekyll, the person who had signed the aforementioned check.

Mr. Utterson determines that "If he could once set eyes on him the mystery would lighten and perhaps roll altogether away. That was the habit of mysterious things when well examined" (20) Therefore, Utterson begins to stake out the door in the rear of Dr. Jekyll's laboratory with the hope of spotting Hyde.

Apart from his relationship with Mr. Enfield, Mr. Utterson is both Dr. Jekyll's lawyer and friend. He is troubled by Enfield's story about the girl being trampled as well as the 'personal will' that Dr. Jekyll had asked him to draft and to be executed in the event of his death: The will states:

> ... in case of the decease of Henry Jekyll, MD, D.C.L., L.L.D., F.R.S., etc., etc., all his possessions were to pass into the hands of his friend and benefactor, Edward Hyde, but that in the case of Dr. Jekyll's disappearance or unexplained absence for any period exceeding three calendar months, the said Edward Hyde should step into the said Henry Jekyll's shoes without further delay and free from any burden or obligation, beyond the payment of a few small sums to the members of the Doctor's household. (16)

Now that Mr. Utterson is aware of additional details about the same Hyde mentioned in the will of Dr. Jekyll, his concern only increases. He visits Dr. Lanyon, a long time friend of Dr. Jekyll, seeking supplemental information on the identity of Mr. Hyde. He is surprised to find out that Dr. Jekyll and Dr Lanyon have had a falling out over philosophical difference. Dr. Lanyon tells Mr. Utterson that Dr. Jekyll had been developing disconcerting ideas, further elaborating that such "unscientific balderdash would estrange Damon and Pythias." (18)

Damon and Pythias are legendary characters in Greek literature that depict the ideal model of friendship. Unlike Utterson and Enfield, and the legendary figures just mentioned, the friendship between Lanyon and Jekyll, which had been very close for several years, could not sustain itself.

The mounting differences between the two men could not be integrated or tolerated. This new development further unnerves Mr. Utterson. He becomes increasingly anxious about Jekyll's personal safety—something he would normally not concern himself with, especially unsolicited.

But again, curiosity is taking hold of his waking thoughts and causing Utterson's to step outside of his normal habits. His ego is being asked to stretch a bit. He subsequently confronts Dr. Jekyll in the following exchange:

> **MR. UTTERSON:** I have been learning something of young Hyde.

The large handsome face of Dr. Jekyll grew pale to the very lips and there came a blackness about his eyes.

> **DR. JEKYLL:** I do not care to hear more. This is a matter I thought we had agreed to drop.

> **UTTERSON:** What I heard was abominable.

Mr. Hyde

JEKYLL: It can make no change. You do not understand my position.

DR. JEKYLL: It is not so bad as that; and just to put your good heart at rest, I will tell you one thing; the moment I choose, I can be rid of Mr. Hyde. (32-33)

The proclamation that Dr. Jekyll can rid himself of Mr. Hyde satisfies Utterson temporarily and seems to reassure Jekyll as well. But this reassurance is only a shallow pretense. Jekyll has, in truth, already begun to feel a mounting uncertainty about his experiment. Why else would he have had Utterson draw up the enigmatic will in the first place if not to placate his rising anxiety?

Unfortunately, this placation only prevents Jekyll from more fully understanding the increasing danger that he will now face. It prevents him from putting up additional psychological guard-rails to protect himself. It precludes him from asking his friend for help. An old saying applies here: "He who has as himself as a patient has as a patient a fool and as a doctor a damn fool." Jekyll is attempting to handle things that have exceeded his abilities.

If, on the other hand, he had confided in Utterson, in full detail, Utterson could have pulled him back from the abyss. Utterson, the good friend that he is, does this to some extent, but without all the facts he is left shortsighted. Jekyll has intentionally not admitted or confessed important information about his experiments. Instead, he mistakenly believes that he can control the situation on his own. He behaves like an addict in the middle stages of an addiction. The defense of denial is operating at its full capacity, and Jekyll, unbeknownst to himself, has already crossed a threshold where the substance, or in this case

Hyde, has gained the upper hand and taken control. While Jekyll maintains his outward persona, his personal shadow, aided by the archetypal shadow, are teaming up as Hyde and growing in exponential strength.

CROSSING THE THRESHOLD

After Jekyll succeeds in opening the door to his more diabolical self, he is not yet aware of what he has created. When he first looked at himself in the mirror, he states:

> I was conscious of no repugnance, rather a leap of welcome. This, too, was myself. It seemed natural and human. In my eyes it bore a livelier image of the spirit, it seemed more expressed and single, than the imperfect and the divine countenance I had been hitherto accustomed to call mine. And in so far, I was doubtless right. I had observed that when I wore the semblance of Edward Hyde, none could come near to me at first without a visible misgiving of the flesh. This, as I take it, was because all human beings, as we meet them, commingled out of good and evil; and Edward Hyde, alone in the ranks of mankind, was pure evil. (102-103)

It is important to note here that pure evil represents not simply a complex. A complex is a mixture of persona, persona shadow, and some archetypal underpinning. Pure Evil, on the other hand, as presented here, manifests itself in its full archetypal force by combining the personal shadow and the archetypal shadow together. Jekyll is now about to experience its effects. The turning point in Stevenson's story occurs when Jekyll goes to sleep as

Jekyll and wakes up as Hyde without having taken the transformative potion. Hyde, growing in power, has found a way to manifest himself under his own will. He no longer needs Jekyll to invite him into existence. In response, Jekyll muses to himself:

> Some two months before the murder of Sir Danvers I had been out for one of my adventures, had returned at a late hour, and woke the next day in bed with somewhat odd sensations. It was in vain I looked about me; in vain I saw the decent furniture and tall proportions of my room in the square; in vain that I recognized the pattern of the bed curtains and the design of the mahogany frame; something still kept insisting that I was not where I was, that I had not awakened where I seemed to be, but in the little room in Soho where I was accustomed to sleep in the body of Hyde. I smiled to myself, and, in my psychological way, began lazily to inquire into the elements of this illusion, occasionally, even as I did so, dropping back into a comfortable morning dose. I was still so engaged when, in one of my more wakeful moments, my eyes fell upon my hand. It was the hand of Edward Hyde. (107)

Jekyll's monologue continues:

> I must have stared upon it for near half a minute, sunk as I was in the mere stupidity of wonder, before terror woke up in my breast and startling as the crash of cymbals, and bounding from my bed, I rushed to the mirror. At the sight that met my eyes, my blood was changed into something exquisitely thin and icy. Yes, I had gone to bed Henry Jekyll, I had awakened Edward Hyde. How was this to be explained? I asked myself;

Hyde's Hand

and then, with another bound of terror—how was it to be remedied? (107-108)

HYDE'S HAND AND ITS SIGNIFICANCE

When Jekyll finally realizes that things have gotten out of control, he decides that he must stop his experiment at once.

He recommits himself to more positive, pro-social activities. He makes use of the psychological defense of undoing, which we will encounter in the story of Dorian Gray in Chapter 12. As a result, Dr. Jekyll, to all outside observers, appears to reverse his direction, and begins to seem like his old self again.

Stevenson writes:

He came out of a self-imposed seclusion and "renewed relationships with his friends, becomes once more their familiar guest and entertainer, and while he was always known for charities, he is now known no less for religion. He was busy, he was much in the open air, he did good; his face seemed to open and brighten, as if with an inward consciousness of service; and for more than two months the doctor was at peace." (53)

Jekyll reflects further:

Strange as the circumstances were, the terms of this debate are as old and commonplace as man; much the same inducements and alarms cast the die for any tempted and trembling sinner; and it fell to me, as it falls with so vast a majority of my fellows, that I chose the better part and was found wanting in the strength to keep it... I made this choice perhaps with some unconscious reservation, for I neither gave up the house in Soho, nor destroyed the clothes of Edward Hyde, which still lay ready in my cabinet. (110)

Wishing away temptation, especially temptation that longs to be satisfied, is a losing cause, especially as Jekyll himself admits above, that he has some "unconscious reservation." This reservation allows Hyde to mount his campaign to re-establish his right to exit. The pressure builds up within Jekyll until, in a moment of vulnerability, Jekyll relapses by taking the transformative potion and the full pent-up force of Hyde, the archetype of Evil, is again released. Hyde is like the genie in the Grimm's fairy tale, *The Spirit in the Bottle.* Once released, it wants to seek revenge for having been caged and contained.

Hyde then commits the murder of Sir Danvers Carew and witnesses confirm to the police that it is indeed Hyde who has committed this horrendous deed. There now ensues a manhunt for Hyde who is now unable to appear in public. He must go into hiding since all of London is on the lookout for him. Even Poole, Jekyll's manservant, would have turned him in, as everyone is still unaware that Jekyll is Hyde and Hyde is Jekyll.

Dr. Jekyll, in desperation, sends a letter to Lanyon, his lifelong friend. Despite their recent differences, he begs Lanyon for his help. This is the first time that Jekyll has asked for help from anyone, as he has reached a point of despair. He now has no control of the transformation process and realizes that he can turn back into Hyde, perhaps permanently, at any moment. Both he as Jekyll, and he, as Hyde, further realize that they are in a difficult situation. Jekyll must find a way to access his dwindling supply of his antidote that is locked away in his laboratory if he is to have any chance at salvation, while Hyde must hide himself from capture.

Jekyll addresses Lanyon in the following letter:

There was never a day when if you had said to me. 'Jekyll, my life, my honor, my reason depends upon you,' I would not have sacrificed my left hand to help you. Lanyon, my life, my honor, my reason, are all at your mercy; if you fail me tonight, I am lost. You might suppose, after this preface, that I am going to ask you to do something dishonorable to grant. Judge for yourself. (84-85)

Jekyll askes Lanyon to go to his laboratory, with instructions of where to look, and to fetch his supply of antidote and to then give it to Hyde who is scheduled to appear at Lanyon's house at midnight that very night. Remember, Hyde is in hiding. He can no longer go to Jekyll's house after Danvers Carew's murder. When Hyde arrives, Lanyon, after a brief interlude, gives Hyde the requested drawer and its contents from Jekyll's laboratory. Hyde is then able to give Lanyon the option to know more about what is really going on or to remain in the dark about the true horror of the situation. Hyde states:

And now, to settle what remains. Will you be wise? Will you be guided? Will you suffer me to take this glass in my hand and go forth from your house without further parley? Or has the greed of curiosity too much command of you? Think before you answer, for it shall be done as you decide. As you decide, you will be left as you were before, and, neither the richer, nor wiser, unless the sense of service rendered to a man in mortal distress may be counted as a kind of riches of the soul. Or, if you so prefer, to choose, a new province of knowledge and new avenues to fame and power shall be laid open to you, here, in this room, upon this instant; and your sight shall be blasted by a prodigy to stagger the unbelief of Satan. (93)

LANYON'S SHOCK AND DEMISE

Laynon replies:

> "I have gone too far in the way of inexplicable services to pause before I see the end." (93)

Dr. Lanyon follows his curiosity and is devastated by what he finds out during this exchange with Hyde—which is that Hyde and Jekyll are one and the same. Lanyon becomes utterly distraught. He isolates himself from the world and withers away and dies within two weeks. Before his last breath, however, he writes and leaves a letter for Utterson to be read upon his death.

THE PRESSURE MOUNTS

Mr. Utterson, re-alarmed by the news of Hyde's murder of Sir Danvers Carew, confronts Dr. Jekyll once again with the following: "One word. Carew was my client, but so are you, and I want to know what I am doing. You have not been mad enough to hide this fellow?" (46)

Jekyll replies,

> Utterson, I swear to God I will never set eyes on him again. I bind my honor to you that I am done with him in this world. It is all at an end. And indeed, he does not want my help; you do not know him as I do; he is safe, he is quite safe; mark my words, he will never more be heard of. (46)

Do these words remind you of an addict who has not quite reached rock bottom? The ego, even when losing its grip, will oftentimes attempt to maintain its sense of still being in control, and during such moments can make ill advised, off balanced decisions. It is not easy, most of the time, for any of us to admit that we need help.

THE ONLY REMAINING SOLUTION

After obtaining his remaining supply of antidote from Lanyon, Jekyll, as himself, is now able to return to his laboratory for self-imposed isolation. But both Jekyll and Hyde, fluctuating between their two selves, began to experience moments of desperation. It is becoming apparently clear that there is no likely equitable way out of their dilemma. Jekyll, on the one hand, can no longer control his experiment. Hyde, on the other hand, is being pursued by the authorities for his murder of Carew. Both are in survival mode with Hyde having the greater desire to preserve himself.

In the meantime, Poole, the housekeeper for Dr. Jekyll, is becoming more and more alarmed for the well-being of his Master. He has heard, and continues to hear all kinds of strange noises, groans, and importunings coming from inside Jekyll's laboratory. All attempts to communicate with his employer inside of the laboratory have been unsuccessful. In a panic Poole seeks out Mr. Utterson's help because he has a growing suspicion that Hyde is in Dr. Jekyll's laboratory and that Hyde may have already harmed or killed Dr. Jekyll. Utterson and Poole break down the door to the laboratory and discovered the following:

Right in the midst there lay the body of a man, sorely contorted and still twitching. They drew near on tiptoe (Utterson and Poole), turned it on its back and beheld the face of Edward

Hyde. He was dressed in clothes far too large for him, clothes of the Doctor's bigness; the cords of his face still moved with a semblance of life, but life was quite gone; and by the crushed vial in his hand and the strong smell of kernels that hung in the air, Utterson knew that he was looking on the body of a self-destroyer. We have come too late, he said sternly, whether to save or to punish. Hyde is gone to his account, and it only remains for us in some manner to find the body of your master. (76-79)

A bit later, after the discovery of Hyde's body, Utterson, back in his office, reads the following letter from Jekyll that has been in Utterson possession—to be read upon the disappearance of Dr. Jekyll.

DR. JEKYLL'S LETTER

I learned to recognize the thorough and primitive duality of man; I saw that, of the two natures that contended in the field of my consciousness, even if I could rightly be said to be either, it was only because I was radically both, and from an early date, even before the course of my scientific discoveries had begun to suggest the most naked possibility of such a miracle, I had learned to dwell with pleasure, as a beloved day-dream, on the separation of these elements. If each, I told myself could but be housed in separate identities, life would be relieved of all that was unbearable; the unjust might go his way, delivered from the aspirations and remorse of his more upright twin, and the just could walk steadfastly and securely on his upward path, doing good things in which he found his pleasure, and no longer exposed to disgrace and penitence by the hands of this extraneous evil. It was the curse of mankind that these incongruous fagots were thus bound together—that in the agonized womb of consciousness, these polar twins should be continuously struggling. (98-99)

Thus, Utterson is finally given all the details and the complete story of his friend's nefarious activities. In a lucid moment Jekyll had killed himself to prevent Hyde from taking over completely. The good had prevailed in the end—but at such an exorbitant cost.

CONCLUSION

If there are indeed polar twins within each of us, struggling for control, a healthy ego, with the help of the Self, or as the alchemists were fond of saying—*Deo Concendente*, God willing, we, as individuals endeavor to do our best to integrate these polarities into a mature and moral person who is not overwhelmed by either pole but, like an awakened Buddha, sitting under the Bodhi tree, able to choose which part of the whole at any given moment is the wholesome action, the wholesome thought, or the wholesome gesture being called for.

This is the wisdom of being awake and present. Without a strong, healthy, and humble ego, the underdeveloped or immature human being is prone to the influence and draw of the pole to which it is most adapted. Consciousness is our only lighthouse in the darkness like Jung's candle and the shadow of the Brocken that he describes in *Memories, Dreams, Reflections*. (87-88)

CHAPTER 10

The Pied Piper and the Problem with the Open Middle

PCL-R score = 4 (normal range)

THE ABILITY TO MAINTAIN a balanced perspective, unhampered by a loss of grounded consciousness, represents the quintessential relational ingredient for the establishment and maintenance of all mutual, trustworthy, and enduring human bonds.

Using the story of the Pied Piper of Hamelin I will examine what happens to individuals or groups who enter relationships and/or agreements when their judging perspective is off-center and unbalanced psychologically. When this happens people enter what I call a 'quick pro quo', a decision made in haste and under duress, versus the healthier *quid pro quo*, which produces an equitable agreement that is beneficial to both parties.

Beginning with the premise that this relational imbalance is ubiquitous, the ideas discussed in this chapter will aid the current efforts to understand the complexity of human relationships and what can lead to unresolved and on-going conflict.

Open Middle

Whenever we are challenged or anxious, there is an ever-present, unconscious tendency, for the ego to be pulled away from what this author refers to as the open middle—that mythical place of focused consciousness exemplified by the Buddha under the Bodhi tree. Here the Buddha sits, in a state of non-attachment, exercising perfect insight, and able to contemplate all areas of the whole universe without becoming overly invested in any one part of it.

Mere human beings, contrasted with the Buddha, are often pulled along, addicted, swallowed up, or simply overwhelmed by life's experiences just as if the gods were pulling invisible puppet strings from above. At such times the archetypal sirens of the psyche, incarnated in sense through the birth of our personal complexes, can and will seduce us with offerings of power, sexual pleasure, false security, unearned wealth and riches, a cloak of indifference, and the promise of eternal youth. These temptations, in turn, can lead us out toward the more extreme poles of any dialectical continuum, and incrementally away from the open middle where there are moderating forces that promote balance.

Stirred to action

Once the neuronal synapses begin to fire in the subconscious parts of our being, however, we are stirred to action. Like characters in a book, the relationship between the protagonist and the antagonist, manifests itself into a building relational tension that catches hold of our attention. Jung (1977), appreciating the dynamics of literary plot and storytelling, saw the same dynamics unfolding in the psyche when he stated that: "… every process is a phenomenon of energy, and that all energy can proceed only from the tension of opposites." (29) This situation happens automatically, through no conscious effort. In fact, it is an established law of physics, a requirement of life, that any action will create an opposite and equal reaction. It is this same dictum of nature that gives birth to the oscillation between dialectical extremes, a phenomenon corresponding to Jung's idea of compensation, an essential feature of the transcendent function.

The transcendent function, in turn, represents a potential to balance out any one-sidedness that has occurred, especially between the conscious and the unconscious, first by allowing, and then holding, the tension that will build up, giving way to the possibility that something new and transformative can be birthed. When this process is observed, and reflected upon, an individual is provided with the base materials to potentially progress along the path to individuation and the fulfillment of his or her authentic destiny. Through this process, we co-create our unique identities in partnership with the Self, the archetype of integration, and with the various other archetypal influences and personal complexes that have come into play.

But, as always, there is the rub. As each of our identities is unique, it makes it impossible for any two of us to share an experience with 100% congruence. While the understanding of a shared event may be close it will never be the same. And while closeness can, but does not always, bring a comforting sense of agreement and safety, distance may, or may not breed suspicion and discord. Furthermore, even when a person is aware of the unsoundness of his or her position, that person may still defend and justify it by finding a rationale that supports their stance, even when on any other day, with clearer vision, such a justification would dissolve under the weight of its own illogic.

Perceived necessity is indeed the mother of invention. Take for example the following quote attributed to Dostoevsky: "When someone flatters you, even when a part of you knows that they are being disingenuous, there is another part of you that wants to believe what they are saying." Obviously, to embrace such flattery, the person being flattered must be willing to distort reality to some degree. It is in the recognizing of this basic human tendency that we can gain the potential to operate from the open middle, the place where truth and wisdom reside. But this, of course, is difficult to do on a consistent basis. Any success will likely be short lived.

Further elaborations

When strong emotions erupt within an individual such as love, anger, rage, hate, jealousy, and fear, this often indicates that a complex is in play. According to Jung complexes are "psychic entities that have escaped from the control of consciousness and split off from it, to lead a separate existence in the dark sphere of the psyche, whence they may at any time hinder or help the conscious performance." (Jacobi, 1973, 36) As a result, a person in complex, may not exercise rational judgment, and more importantly, his or her perceived middle is likely to be left or right of the actual true center to begin with. Furthermore, once the crisis is over, the ego can shift back seamlessly to a more favorable advantage point without skipping a beat and quickly deny that it was ever in any other place. This tendency to shift away from the open middle is an omnipresent human defense dynamic that I will now explore in the story of the Pied Piper of Hamelin.

THE PIED PIPER: *Solve et Coagula*

Robert Browning (1842/1993), one of many writers who make use of the legend of the Pied Piper, begins his historic poem with the following lines:

> Hamelin Town's in Brunswick, by the famous Hanover City.
> The river Weser, deep and wide,
> washes its wall on the Southern side.
> A pleasanter spot you never spied.
> but, when begins my ditty,
> Almost five hundred years ago,
> To see townsfolk, suffer so from vermin,
> was a pity. (6)

These lines poise the collective problem faced by the citizens of Hamelin, namely that their town is plagued with an infestation of rats. In our own time there are similar fears of an Ebola outbreak, mutating strains of the Covid 19 virus, the continuing effects of racial injustice, economic inequality, the push for acceptance of multiple sexual identities beyond traditional heterosexuality, a corrupt justice system, and the rigidity of religious fundamentalism. There is, as well, a growing tension between citizens and the police, centered on the abuse of power. We are separated into Red and Blue States, as well as numerous other classifications that can distort our perspective and shift us away from the open middle.

This shift is further aided by a tendency on the part of the masses to look to those in power to solve their problems and thereby abdicating their part in a collective responsibility. This dynamic diminishes the individual. It relieves a person of his or her personal responsibility and results in various negative consequences that are well documented in places like Nazi Germany, the My Lai massacre, Iran, China, Russia, the Catholic Church's handling of the sexual abuse of children, and in Milgram's experiments in the early 1960s.

Milgram tested the extent that college students were willing to abdicate their own decision-making agency to obey the orders of an authority figure. In this experiment the student was asked to administer increasing levels of electric shock to another indivudal who was an actor. The actor pretended to experience increasing amounts of pain as the voltage was increased. Milgram found that most students were willing to obey the authority figure, even though to do so caused them some discomfort.

These dynamics are all present in the story of the Pied Piper. The people have abdicated their personal responsibility and the mayor, along with his Council, have behaved irresponsibly while enjoying the benefits, perks, and advantages of office. Simply put they have not followed through on their sworn duties and campaign promises. When pressed by the town's citizens for a solution to the rat problem the town leaders look for convenient scapegoats and utilize one excuse after the other to let themselves off the hook. By avoiding responsibility, however, they simply kick the can down the proverbial road. In mounting desperation, the town's folk shout out:

To think we buy gowns lined with ermine,

for dolts that can't or won't determine

What's best to rid us of our vermin!

You hope, because you're old and obese,

To find in the furry civic robes your ease.

Rouse up, Sirs! Give your brains a racking

To find the remedy we're lacking,

Or, sure as fate,

we'll send you packing! (23)

THE SYMBOLISM OF RATS

At this point it seems important to ask: What is the symbolism of rats? They are, after all, an intricate part of the story. Although rats can symbolize various things in different cultures, in the European mindset in which the story occurs "the rat is regarded in folk belief as the personification of illnesses, witches, demons, and goblins" (Herder, 1993, 156). Furthermore, "There is a rat or mouse element within many of us: a small, feral, chthonic aspect of ourselves reprehensible in the eyes of the collective." (*Book of Symbols*, 292) Also, "Notorious as hosts of the fleas that spread Bubonic Plaque to the millions of people in the Middle Ages (and also killed millions of rats) they are mythic harbingers of scourge." (292).

Given the above amplification we find the town of Hamelin, once prosperous and abundantly blessed, currently infested with a Creature that can "...gnaw its way through just about anything, including brick, wood, and lead." (Book of Symbols, 290). We find those in power hard-pressed and fearful yet not wise enough to gnaw through their own incompetence to exercise good judgment. With mounting emotions, things cannot go on as they are. As the tension builds how will it all get resolved? Will the rats take over? Will a solution be found to subjugate the rats? Will human and rat become indifferent to each other or strike a compromise? Will a miracle occur that re-establishes a balance between the otherwise antagonistic parties? It is all up in the air. There is no apparent guiding source in the story that is inclined to move to the open middle where genuineness, authenticity, integrity, and wisdom reside. And even if such a guiding source presented itself, would it be heeded?

It is also important to note something I stated earlier—that once an ego that has been hard-pressed and fearful is no longer backed into a corner, it can and will change its position. Thus, the center of consciousness is not an absolute set point always tethered to an authentic middle, but rather a point that vacillates to meet the present, felt needs of the ego.

I recall that when studying the Myers-Brigg Type Inventory that most results do not indicate a perfect balance between the four dialectical positions, namely Introvert/Extrovert, Sensation/ Intuition, Thinking/Feeling, and Perception /Judgment. In fact, terms such as superior or inferior position readily indicate that people are not balanced but instead have certain proclivities that pull them one way or the other in a mild, moderate, or extensive manner. And so perhaps this notion of the open middle, or the Buddha sitting peacefully under the Bodhi tree, is a somewhat idealistic notion, though we oftentimes strive for the ideal.

THE PIED PIPER / AN AGREEMENT MADE UNDER DURESS
As the City Council hides in its chamber to avoid the growing frustration of the citizens there is a knock on the Council door.

When the door is opened, in walks a strange figure. Browning (1842/1993) describes him in the following way:

His queer long coat from heel to head
was half of yellow and half of red.
And he himself was tall and thin,
with sharp blues eyes, each like a pin. (27)

Upon entry the Piper stated:
And, if it please your honors,
I am able by means of a secret charm, to draw all Creatures living
beneath the sun, that creep,
or swim,
or fly,
or run!
And I chiefly use my charm on creatures that do people harm,
the mole, and the toad, and newt, and viper,
and people call me the Pied Piper. (29)

With the Council's undivided attention, the Piper further states:
"If I can rid your town of rats, will you give me a thousand guilders?
(32)

The Council, in unison, exclaimed:
"One? We will give you fifty thousand!"

So, while the Piper has asked for the reasonable fee of 1,000 guilders, he is promised 50,000, and the deal is struck. But herein lies the problem. The deal is negotiated under conditions of duress. One could easily ask: Is the city council competent to enter into such an agreement? Do they understand the ramifications of such a deal and the financial liability that will be incurred by the city?

Today, in the news, we are apt to hear multiple stories about individuals admitting to or agreeing to things while under duress or interrogation. We read reports about the extraction of information from alleged terrorists, or detainees in jail, through the unethical practice of torture. We also find that while the results of such activities and practices may be highly satisfying at the time, at least to those involved, the conclusions reached are distorted and bare little semblance to the truth. There is an imbalance at play in all these situations.

A quick review of Heraclitus' concept of *enantiodromia* may be helpful in highlighting the point I wish to make. Heraclitus stated that "If something goes far enough in one direction it will end up in its opposite." The situation in Hamlin is like a loan shark lending money to a desperate individual who has little potential to repay the loan and will grow increasingly angry over time for having agreed to such a loan in the first place.

In striking such an inflated deal I believe that the Piper is also just as culpable as the city council. He is either unable or unconcerned about setting and insisting on a fair price for his services. Recalling the adage, 'Whatever the market will bear.' The Piper simply accepts the outlandish deal because that is what is being offered. This greedy mentality perpetuates an in-balance that will need to be corrected. It sets up the experience of having been treated unfairly and this, like any injustice, will lead to a subsequent desire to retaliate, to correct the imbalance.

As I reflected on this dynamic, I was reminded of Riane Eisler's book, *The Chalice and the Blade* (1995). Eisler described two basic models for society. She states:

> The first, which I call the dominator model, is what is popularly termed either patriarchy or matriarchy—the ranking of one half of humanity over the other. The second, in which social relations are primarily based on the principle of linking rather than ranking, may best be described as the partnership model. In this model—beginning with the most fundamental differences in our species, between male and female, diversity is not equated with either inferiority or superiority. (xvii)

The dominator model seems to fit quite well with the Darwinian idea about the 'survival of the fittest.' It also fits and supports both Freud's notion that we seek pleasure as well as Adler's concept of 'will to power.' This model reinforces the ego's desire to seek out what pleases it and establishes the importance of hierarchy and status to feel secure and to obtain what one wants. This sense of ascendancy over the other, manifests in quotidian statements such as my dog is bigger than your dog, my school is more elite than your school, my skin is lighter than your skin, and the patriarchal favorite 'might makes right!'

HAMELIN

The town of Hamelin, once prosperous and thriving before the rat infestation, may well have dominated its neighbors. All these advantages, however, seem to address superficialities and monetary concerns and not the deeper potentials that can only be discovered and developed once a certain level of safety and security, and trustworthiness, have been achieved. Eisler reminds us that safety and security can only be achieved through cooperation not domination. Her research shows that human beings can work together for the collective good without need of hierarchy, elitism, and or/any other kind of dominance over those who are less endowed. She would, I believe, endorse the Arthurian concept of the round table and the accompanying idea that Lancelot was not the leader, or the best knight, but instead "the first among equals." The partnership model recognizes both strengths and weaknesses and provides a place at the table for everyone's contribution, however humble. It debunks the absolutism of Darwin's "survival of the fittest."

THE STORY CONTINUES...

The Piper, with contract in hand, leaves the Council Chamber and proceeds to the City Square. He commences to play a magical tune on his pipe. As he plays rats emerge from every kind of abode and hiding place and begin to follow the Piper as he walks toward the South Gate of the City. Passing through the City Gate the Piper approaches the flowing river Weser and slowly wades into its water, all the while continuing to play his pipe.

The rats, operating under the spell of his enchanting music, not unlike a person under the sway of a complex, all jump into the river and drown as they are swept away in the current. All perish except for one rat who miraculously swims to the other side. His survival now represents the potential residing within the rat psyche to learn from his experiences and to pass such learning to his brother and sister rats living elsewhere. So, yes, even the rats, who are lured by their rat sirens and their rat complexes can exhibit an inchoate capacity to become conscious and to learn from their experience. But will they? Instead of just avoiding Hamelin altogether, will they come to a deeper (conscious or instinctual) understanding of what has led to their demise in the first place? History suggests not, for both rats and humankind.

BROKEN AGREEMENT

With his job completed the Piper returns to collect his fee on July 22nd, 1376. But with the rats removed and the crisis over the attitude of the mayor, city council, and the people of Hamelin has shifted. Rationalizing that the Piper has really done nothing other than apparently played a simple tune on his pipe the Council now refuses to honor the contract that they have agreed to, namely a payment of $50,000 guilders. They try to simply dismiss the Piper. They will not pay the 50,000 guilders. They will not even pay the original 1,000 guilders that the Piper had initially proposed. They will offer instead only an insulting figure of fifty guilders. If the Piper refuses, they threaten to lock him up for bothering them with his continuous importuning.

The Piper, having his own complexes, senses an injustice and does not maintain his balance or composure. Instead, he reacts like most human beings would. He seeks out redress for his predicament. He gives the city 24 hours to reconsider this stalemate and promises to return the next day for their decision. When he returns the city maintains its refusal. The Piper abruptly leaves the Council chambers only to return the next day wearing an all-red hat, a symbol of his rage. The Piper then proceeds to play another mysterious tune on his pipe, only this time, instead

The Pied Piper and the Children

of rats, all the children of the town become mesmerized by the music and are led away just as the rats had been lead away two days before. Rather than drowning the children in the river, however, the Piper leads them up a mountainside path and they quickly disappear into an opening in the side of the mountain. This opening subsequently shuts itself up again disallowing anyone to follow. This obliterates the future of Hamelin because the children, in essence, carry the hopes and the dreams of their parents into the near future. Without them there is no next generation, no future. There is, however, another wrinkle in the story. Just as there had been a previous survivor among the rats, one child is left behind as well.

Browning (1842/1993) writes:

As if a cavern was suddenly hollow.
And the Piper advanced and the children followed,
And when all were in to the very last,
The door in the mountainside shut fast.
Did I say all? No! One was lame,
And could not dance the whole of the way.
And in the after years if you would blame his sadness, he used to say, --
It is dull in our town since my playmates left!
I can't forget that I'm bereft
Of all the pleasant sights they see
Which the Piper also promised me.
For he led us, he said, to a joyous land,
Joining the town and just at hand,
Where waters gushed and fruit trees grew,
And flowers put forth a fairer hue

And everything was strange and new.
The sparrows were brighter than peacocks here,
And their dogs outran our fellow deer,
And honeybees had lost their sting,
And horses were born with eagles' wings.
And just as I became assured
My lame foot would be speedily cured,
The music stopped and I stood still,
And found me outside the Hill,
Left alone against my will,
To go now limping as before,
And never hear of that country more!

As we can see, the sole survivor is not a transformed soul or the Buddha. He is looking instead, like any predictable ego, for a fairytale ending. He longs for what he doesn't have and fails to make use of what he has just experienced. Unknown to the inchoate ego, it is looking in the wrong place. The place he looks seduces him (and all of us) into once again believing that there is a Shangri-La or as Browning states: "a joyous land", or the place that Moses sought, namely, a land flowing with milk and honey. We seem always too willing to fall for the instant gratification that promises to soothe us. This willingness to be seduced subtly keeps us captive, and like the surviving rat, unlikely to learn the larger lesson that is being taught.

IN CONCLUSION

The real gold in the story is apparently hiding. It is hiding in the very thing that both the rat and the child survivor want to avoid, namely honesty, fair play, balance, and harmony. Both rat and human need to embrace all parts of their whole instead of chasing after only those parts of the whole that seem desirous. But as has been said earlier we oftentimes seek the easy way out of any perceived difficulty. In our laziness we deny the more shadowy and disagreeable parts of ourselves and ignore the reflective consciousness of the open middle.

By doing so we render ourselves particularly vulnerable to the Piper's tune. This doesn't mean that all is lost, however. The gold is simply returned to the unconscious, into the closed side of the mountain, much as Excalibur was returned to the Lady of the Lake when Arthur lay dying. It will remain at rest until such a time that it can be accessed by the next individual hero, or heroine, awake enough to note its presence.

The Golem

CHAPTER 11

THE GOLEM

Individuation and Transcendence

PCL-R score = 3 (Normal range)

THE STORY OF THE Golem, which predates and perhaps anticipates Frankenstein's Creature, is a parable about the potential individuation process and the development of the whole individual. It addresses, with perspicacity, the unforeseen current problems with Artificial Intelligence (AI) and the concept of ex-machina, when something transforms, naturally, or through mutation, into something beyond its original intended limits.

The Golem story emerges from the cabbalist tradition of Jewish mysticism, and true to its symbolic nature, there isn't just one tale of the Golem—there are many. Each, like the various characters in the film *Roshomon* (Kurosawa, 1950), provides another snapshot into a myriad of underlying themes out of which we attempt to understand the truth. Since one's perspective is uniquely individual it will be largely shaped by one's psychological vantage point, which can be from a mountaintop, from a raft adrift in the ocean, or from the belly of the large fish, to name but a few places. Each place, being constructed from parts available, will have certain advantages and disadvantages. Furthermore, when working with powerful mystical elements, some of which may cause unexpected consequences, it is essential to honor these energies and take the necessary precautions to prevent falling victim to a state of inflation. Inflation is amply exemplified by the adage: power corrupts, and absolute power corrupts absolutely.

POWER

The seduction of power, the need for control, and the effects of both Good and Evil, have all, given rise to the repeated themes found in fairy tales of all cultures. Each theme, in turn, serves as a lesson about what can happen when a dialectical dialogue goes awry. To prevent this from happening there must be a structure to contain and manage such energies. A certain humility must first be in place, however, whereby one does not exceed his or her level of competency. Some containers, are of course, better than others in holding this tension. This tension, none the less, is a prerequisite for any idea to become animated and alive. Without such a spark (élan vital) all remains fallow and impotent. The actor or observer, astute or ignorant, is perpetually invited to apprehend the symbolic —to increase, by a smidgin, the wisdom birthed out of human consciousness, and human experience. But with something so ephemeral, present, and available one second, that something can be gone in a proverbial flash, just like a dream image. Furthermore, the powerful, ego-based individual, prone to act in haste, will often fail to comprehend what the 'dummling' (von Franz, 1996, 46), or less ego-driven individual, simply stumbles upon. According to Christ after all, "unless you turn around and be like children, you will never enter the kingdom of heaven (Matthew, Chapter 18, Verse3/4). I believe that this instruction from Christ suggests that a pinch of humility is always a prerequisite to authentic success. For the secrets of the universe will often otherwise conceal themselves, or if apprehended at all, lead to your downfall when your ego claims too much credit for any such blessing or windfall.

A FINE BALANCE

In seeking knowledge, wisdom, and self-growth, humans, as a species, always seem to be poised on a teeter totter, attempting a fine balance between the dark abyss and the call to their teleological potential. The undisciplined pilgrim proceeds one step ahead and then takes two steps back. He or she will find that the road forward is a circular path rather than a linear one. If the journeyer learns this lesson they can make progress, and the journey can proceed. According to Jung "there is no linear evolution; there is only a circumambulation of the self." (1973, 196) Like the underlying meaning of the cliché, 'he or she has been around the block,' wisdom and understanding can develop—but only with repeated exposure to life, and with the addition of some degree of integration. Without integration we simply walk in a same sized circle. With integration, the circle is enlarged into an expanding spiral. Yet even then, development doesn't just occur as a matter of course. It requires continuous reflection and conscious tending for Jung's concept of individuation is indeed an act against nature (an *opus contra natura*). Jung (1954) states "The aim of individuation is nothing less than to divest the self of the false wrappings of the persona on the one hand, and the suggestive power of the primordial image on the other." (174) These false wrappings and experiences of inflated power resonate with Levy-Bruhl's concept of participation mystique (Jung, 1984, 31). Power can pull any of us into a womb-like collective, be it the collective conscious (persona-bound, group think, the latest fashion, dogma) or into the collective unconscious (psychosis, possession). The result is always predictable because it follows a collective, archetypal pattern, not an individual one. Stagnation, or in-authenticity will manifest in the former case, while potential destruction, at its worse, will arise in the latter instance. Against such titans, the spark of individuation is often fragile and vulnerable. This spark is at risk for extinction, a risk described by Jung in his autobiography *Memories, Dreams, Reflections* (1989) when he states:

> Suddenly, I had the feeling that something was coming up behind me. I looked back and saw a gigantic black figure following me. But at the same moment I was conscious, that in spite of my terror, I must keep my little light going through night and wind, regardless of all dangers. When I awoke, I realized at once that the figure was a specter of the Brocken, my own shadow on the swirling mists, brought into being by the little light that I was carrying. I knew, too, that this little light was my consciousness, the only light I have. My own understanding is the sole treasure I possess, and the greatest. Though infinitely small and fragile in comparison to the powers of darkness, it is still a light, my only light. (88)

Unfortunately, for many, if their light is extinguished, there may never be a second chance to get it right. For those who are still alive and kicking, however, and for those whose spark still beckons, Beowulf's (1957) counsel continues to be apropos: "Unless a man is doomed, fortune is apt to favor the man who keeps his nerve." (17)

To be favored in the way that Beowulf suggests means to heed the call to individuate, to become more whole. Out of the tensions of the opposites, if the tension is held, a third possibility, representing something new and refreshing arises. Notably, this process parallels a major tenet of alchemy: One becomes two, two becomes three, and out of the third comes the one as the fourth (Axiom of Maria, Jung, CW 12, 26). Similarly, from the Secret of the Golden Flower, Wilhelm (1931) writes: "The spirit is thought; thought is heart; the heart is fire; the fire is the Elixir." (39)

All the above parts are necessary if a critical mass is to be achieved. If one part is missing or underdeveloped, or weighted to one side, the potential excitement of the "lesser coniunctio will fail to maintain its promise and a hole will develop in the container, allowing energy to escape, thus preventing the process from completing itself. Fulfillment of its promise, on the other hand, will lead to the "greater *coniunctio*" which results in the summation of the parts into a unified new whole. The lesser *coni⁻unctio* is like the idea of giving a man a fish to feed him for a day. It's a placeholder that works for the moment but is not transfor-mational, like when you teach a man to fish – the greater *coni⁻unctio*. That is a gift that represents real growth toward autonomy —a gift that can be carried into the future.

Meyrink hinted at the process of individuation, and of course, to other possible paths that can befall an individual in his book the *Golem* (1925). He writes: "According to tradition, three men once descended into the Realm of Darkness; one went mad; the other lost his sight, and only the third returned safe and sound, and related that he had met himself." (74) This third man had received the gift of wholeness, the gift of being himself.

The process of individuation, of course, is never an easy one. It is fraught with many obstacles and challenges. On such a path some individuals inevitably go mad while others get swallowed by the collective and lose their authentic voice. Recall the biblical verse "Many are called but few are chosen" (Matthew, 22:14).

How The Rabbi manages inflation

In all myths, the hero does not succeed simply because he or she is brave, strong, or intelligent. Instead, success occurs because there is something present, an influence, a god or goddess, or an unconscious nudge, that assists to push the desired outcome in a particular direction. This idea of divine intervention, especially in difficult times, resonates in the phrase "God is on our side," a phrase that can ground us in humility as well as inflate us with arrogance. Indeed, all heroes must manage the inevitable hubris that results from a relationship with the granting power. Otherwise, each hero will meet the same fate as Icarus.

The story of Icarus "symbolizes limitless and unreasonable adventuresomeness." (Herder, 1986, 104). To avoid such a fate Icarus needed simply to follow the instructions of his father Daedalus. These instructions are given with the best of intentions, to keep Icarus safe and secure. But as we can see throughout the history of humankind, following such instructions is not an easy task. Successful heroes are the exception—not the rule, just as successful individuation is an exception and not the guaranteed outcome of anyone's life. As we will notice, with the creation of the Golem, there are indeed instructions to be followed, and human weaknesses and temptations to be manage and overcome.

CREATION (NEW LIFE)

The Maharal, attuned to the sufferings of his congregation, refuses to submit to the unjust cruelty being visited upon his people. Although seemingly impotent before the immensity of Evil, he choses to question the inevitability of such suffering and seeks out another possibility. Using mystical rituals into which he has been initiated, he formulates the question he wants to ask in a dream (Wiesel, *The Golem*, 44), the dream being an avenue to communicate with God.

The Rabbi asks: "How can I protect my people?" The Rabbi receives the following answer in his dream. (Chayim Bloch, 1925, 66)

Ato Bra Golem Devuk Hakhomer

V'tigzar Zedim Chevel Torfe Yisroel

[Make a Golem of clay and you will destroy the entire Jew-baiting company.]

The answer from the dream represents a gift from the unconscious, a gift that the Rabbi's conscious ego humbly accepts and integrates.

Blood Libel

One major historical example of how conflict and projected shadow have manifested over the years between Jew and Gentile is the ubiquitous allegation by Christians that Jews, who usually lived in a separate section of a city, referred to as the Ghetto, secretly conspired to kidnap and kill Christian children for the purpose of using the victim's blood in the making of Passover matzos. These accusations were hard for a Jewish person to defend against, despite only circumstantial or manufactured evidence to justify the said arrest and conviction.

The Rabbi sets out to create a being that can balance out the odds, correct the injustices that were occurring, and give his people a better chance of survival. Such were the superstitions and conditions in Prague in the Sixteenth century, although in truth, these imaginings differ very little from some of the present day beliefs that different groups have of each other. The sway of fake news, among other things, creates a climate in which facts are hard to discern. People, in turn, can act upon false premises and oftentimes do great harm. Sincere ignorance can flame the worst atrocities. A 'cancel culture' can cancel out and persecute a person who does not adhere to the current dogma or psychological paradigm. It seems that "we" like to project the undesirable not only onto our adversaries but also onto the unsuspecting scapegoat who, at convenient times, serves to protect us from some disturbing aspect within ourselves. According to Perera (1979)

> Scapegoating, as it is practiced, means finding the one or ones who can be identified with evil or wrongdoing, blamed for it, and cast out from the community in order to leave the

remaining members with feelings of guiltlessness, atoned and at one with the collective standards of behavior (9).

Then, in the days before enlightenment, as now, during the so-called scientific era, the presence of the devil and of Evil remain palpable—thus ensuring the conditions that foster the unconscious use of projection. That said, Perera further reminds us that "Ultimately, we may be restored to a sense of wholeness by enduring the conflict and bringing the polarized opposites to consciousness, thus activating what Jung called the transcendent function" (1979, 12)

Enduring the conflict was what Christ called us to do when he suggested "Do not set yourself against the man who wrongs you. If someone slaps you on the right cheek, turn and offer your left." (Matthew, 5:39) Holding the tension at such a moment and not striking back can allow for the aforementioned "third" possibility to arise, namely the insight that the person being struck may not be the enemy. Such an insight can occur in that timeless moment when one is expecting a counterattack but the person who has been struck does not retaliate. This hesitation can create an opportunity.

In Bloch's version of the Golem, Rabbi Loew follows his divine instructions to the letter. He is a man who possesses great humility and recognizes his own limitations. He credits the source of his power to God, instead of succumbing to the temptation of self-aggrandizement. He understands that he will need the help of others, including God, to harness and manage the divine energies. His statement to his two companions who assist him to create the Golem parallel the Axiom of Maria and its equivalent from the Secret of the Golden Flower. Rabbi Loew exhorts:

I wish to make a Golem, and beg your assistance, for this creation requires four elements: Aysch, Mayim, Ruach, and Aphar (fire, water, air, and earth). Thou Isaac art the element of fire; thou Jakob art water; I am air. Together, we shall render the fourth element, earth, the Golem. (Bloch, 66).

And then... at daybreak four men went homeward (Bloch, 69). Here, the word *beg*, as well as the request for assistance is most important. They attest to an attitude of humility and the recognition of a higher authority. The ego, so to speak, goes to one knee and reaches to kiss the ring of the king. Such character is woefully absent in the creation tales of Dr. Jekyll and Mr. Hyde and Victor Frankenstein, discussed in earlier chapters. Jung, however, constantly underscored the importance of such an attitude (humility) and recognized the fallibility and limits of his and humankind's knowledge. This recognition is spotlighted when Jung quotes Ignatius Loyola in the following statement:

"Man's consciousness was created to the end that it may 1) recognize its descent from a Higher authority; 2) pay due and careful regard to this source; 3) execute its commands intelligently and responsibly; and 4) thereby afford the psyche as a whole the optimum degree of life and development." (CW9, ¶253)

So yes, the ego has a very important part to play in life, on that there is no dispute. But the ego is not the prime mover of things. Instead, one must have the right attitude to be the right person to succeed in the heroic endeavor. A quote by an ancient adept states: "if the wrong man uses the right method, the right means will work in the wrong way."

TWISTS AND TURNS

In Wegener's 1920 black and white movie about the Golem, Rabbi Judah Loew, depicted in 1580 Prague, constructs a Creature made of clay. The original purpose of this Creature has been often debated, but most seem to favor the idea that the Golem was to be an everyday servant to the Rabbi. He was to perform household tasks, study the Torah, and to simply do the Rabbi's bidding. Selfless servitude. No one else, however, was to direct or manage this man made of clay. Other versions of the story claim that the Golem possessed supernatural powers and that his main purpose was loftier and more important than just menial chores. First among these loftier tasks was to protect the Jewish people living in the ghetto from the larger non—Jewish populace. I prefer this latter purpose because it seems to be a better use of sacred energy, protecting the people, contrasted to the first suggested use of the Golem as a house servant doing common chores. I believe that the Golem, in many ways, represents a concretized representation of Rabbi Loew's inner state of transcendence.

A SOURCE OF TENSION AND PROJECTION

In Prague, in the sixteenth century, the Jews and the Christians represent a classic example of a 'tension of the opposites.' It is very similar to today's clashes between blue states versus red states, democrats versus republicans, Palestinians versus Israelis, communist versus capitalists, Jungians versus Freudians, and on and on. Each side of the opposition conveniently carries the projected shadow of the other side. And while conflict between distinct groups is inevitable, Jung and others have stated on multiple occasions that the first step toward individuation is to take back one's projections. According to Jung "the supreme aim of the opus psychologicum is conscious realization, and the first step is to make oneself conscious of the contents that have hitherto been projected." (Jung, CW 16, ¶471). Furthermore, Jacobi, in discussing Jung, states:

> In such cases everything of which the individual is unaware in his own psyche is projected onto the object, and if he fails to recognize the projected content in himself, he makes a scapegoat of the object. The ethical task confronting him is to discern in himself the opposed attitudinal habitus, which is structurally present in everyone. By consciously accepting and developing it, the individual would not only achieve balance for himself but improve his understanding of his fellow man. (1973, 21).

Withdrawing your projections is also the whole premise of Erik Neuman's book entitled *Depth Psychology and the New Ethic* (1990). He identifies projection as a convenient way to avoid responsibility by blaming others. Neuman (1990) states "whatever is denied and disowned at home is discovered in another person or group and there seen as inferior and subhuman, the villain, the enemy." (3)

The old ethic allows all of us to believe that we can be all good, and that the other side can be all bad. How convenient! The new ethic, however, doesn't afford such comfort. Instead, it demands that we take responsibility for the good as well as the bad within each of us. In the context of the Golem story, the Christian community possesses the political clout and the superior numbers to exercise secular, extroverted power. The

Jewish community, on the other hand, while not outwardly powerful, maintains its traditions and separateness, and thus retains its introverted identity and internal authority. Both sides, however, inevitably projected onto the other. As a result, each side held an important piece essential to the other's potential growth.

A LARGER TRUTH

The creation of the Golem represents, symbolically, the ability to transcend human frailty and to discover a larger truth about ourselves and the "other." For example, when a Jew was unjustly accused of some invented crime, the individuated Rabbi, or perhaps the Golem, possessed an ability to see into the hearts of the false accuser and to find the weakness in the accusation—thus bringing the light of justice to bare upon the legal proceedings and correcting what had been a staged judicial farce.

WIESEL'S GOLEM

Eli Wiesel (1983) gives a brief description of the Golem:

> To us he was a savior. Though mute and unhappy, a savior was what he was. Nobody understood him because no one was like him. Do you know anyone who lives only for others, who devotes his every breath, his every thought, every inch of his being to a single, sacred purpose: to protect the life, the security, and the future of the community. He was said to be a fool, I know. They say he was stupid, backward. I do not agree. He was a saint. (12)

Of course, one problem with the above description is the suggestion that the Golem was in some way unhappy. Why would a Golem be unhappy? Could this state of unhappiness be the result of one-sidedness? Should the devotion given to others also be balanced by a devotion to self—at least in the sense of understanding one's own needs and not being afraid or hesitant to take care of your whole being? Might the Golem long for additional development beyond the mere capacity to serve the Rabbi? In a robot there is no apparent capacity to consider more than what is programmed, but how about a Creature endowed with apparent human thoughts and feelings?

APPROACHING CREATION

In constructing the Golem (in the 1920 movie) Rabbi Loew first had to obtain the magical word from the dreaded dark spirit Astaroth. In dealing with such a spirit there are always inherent dangers. For example, Loew must place himself in a position of uncertainty and peril, conditions created by proximity to the dark power Astaroth. Loew's motivations, however, are pure and altruistic and his actions are based on a genuine desire to protect others as the leader of the Jewish community. His knowledge on how to proceed is also key. It represents a blessing birthed directly from his faith in God. It is not a product of hubris as is the case with both Drs. Jekyll and Victor Frankenstein.

Let us now hear and sense the humility in Rabbi Loew (Singer, 1982) during a conversation with a stranger, who is actually an emissary from God. Rabbi Loew is afraid that the Christians are planning a pogrom over some recent false allegations. In a humble manner he seeks guidance. Loew asked the stranger:

What should we do? He includes the collective "we" and not the egoistic "I." The stranger replies:

> Make a Golem of clay. You will engrave one of God's names on the Golem's forehead, and with the power of that sacred name he will live for a time and do his mission. His name will be Joseph. But take care that he should not fall into the follies of flesh and blood. (23)

The Rabbi is human, however, along with all that that entails. If he does not abuse this trust that has been placed in him, as might a lesser mortal, the blessings will continue. By sticking to the pre-ordained plan, the dark power/energy is contained. The Rabbi draws a magic circle around himself, a temenos, to protect himself as he negotiates with Astaroth. Despite all the effort to control potential dangers, i.e., the best laid plans *Of Mice and Men* (Steinbeck, 1994) such dangers or dark energies can still get their chance to exert an influence in the story in unexpected ways. After all the psyche doesn't take sides. It does not, sorry to say, organically favor one end of the continuum of Good and Evil over the other.

SOMETHING IMPURE

In Leivick's (1921) play entitled *The Golem*, the reader is alerted about the potential interplay between dark and light energies right at the beginning of the play. The Maharal, Rabbi Loew, states: "Something impure has invaded what I strove so hard to render holy. With words of fear, I myself produced a flaw within the heart to be." (11) This flaw apparently manifests in the Golem's desire to become human, to exceed his designed capacity. Like today's movies about automatons developing human characteristics, desires, and tendencies, this momentary 'something impure' allows space for the follies of flesh and blood to stake a claim and exert an influence. Perhaps, however, such an allowance is part of nature's overall plan.

While the purpose of the Rabbi's efforts is to protect the Jewish people, the Golem begins to have human feelings and desires, and this opens the door to additional longings and human development—something that is never straightforward or streamlined. This inevitably includes the need to be loved and to seek companionship (like Frankenstein's Creature). This additional need will compete with and disrupt his central, superior function.

In the end of Levick's play, the Golem becomes enthralled with the Rabbi's daughter, and like Lenny in Steinbeck's (1994) novel, of Mice and Men, he is ill-equipped to deal with the multiple levels of human interaction. His struggle to understand his feelings outpace his ability to comprehend. The Golem in Leivick's story, during an upsurge of emotion, envelopes the Rabbi's daughter in an asphyxiating embrace and unintentionally kills her, like Lenny's embrace of the rabbits in Steinbeck's book *Of Mice and Men*. This is certainly an unintentioned outcome.

CLAY

Clay is the substance from which the Golem is constructed. It is a chthonic substance—from out of the earth. When I looked up "clay" in the symbol dictionary (Herder, 1978) I was referred to the word <u>container</u>. A container can be defined as "a symbol of receiving and holding, and thus frequently a symbol of the womb."

Christianity compares Mary, who received the Holy Ghost into herself, with a container. A container, particularly one made of clay, is also the symbol for body, which is interpreted as the container of the soul. The New Testament compares the believer to a container of Grace. Many people considered the pouring of a liquid from one container into another as a symbol of reincarnation of the soul. (46)

After it is created, the Golem performs to Rabbi Loew's specifications and directions.

Wiesel (1983) described the Golem in the following way: "His bearing was awkward and astonishingly agile. Riveted to the ground but floating in the air. Strange, mysterious, he seemed to plow earth and heaven all at once." (32)

Thus, the Golem seemed in possesseion of super abilities emanating from below and above coming from and including all parts of the whole. These abilities allowed the Golem to do such things as to make himself invisible, to withstand insults, to converse with wondering spirits, and to see through walls and into men's thoughts. Wiesel (1983) further stated:

> Since he never talked, and since he always seemed to surprise you, to shock you, to force you out of the ordinary, to break your habits, some people would get impatient with him. But he, like a sleeping or walking statue, exhibited total indifference. Almost unapproachable, he allowed no one to offend him. If he were ridiculed, he ignorned it. If stones were thrown at him, he did not react. There was almost no way of getting him angry. Only the godless enraged him; his brothers could do anything. Despite what you think, he was not less human than we, but more human. (34)

OVER TIME

Over time, the Golem as depicted in the 1920 movie, becomes increasingly erratic and uncontrollable. Rabbi Loew learns that it is in the Golem's nature to turn on his creator, especially when the Golem is given life beyond his intended purpose. For example, the Rabbi's wife wants the Golem to take care of the multiple mundane daily chores around the house. She argues with her husband—Why not? Why shouldn't we take advantage of his strength and energy to make our lives a little less menial?

While the Rabbi is tempted to indulge his wife's wishes, as they have some merit, he holds out and refuses. Loew subsequently decides to decommission the Golem by removing the secret word from the amulet on the Golem chest—the secret to its animation. Loew does this because he knows that he is being tempted to misuse the Golem and to thereby go beyond his instructions from God.

He exercises good sound judgment represented by good ego control and the presence of wisdom. He is thus able to manage the situation—unlike what we saw with Dr. Jekyll earlier. Unfortunately, Loew's assistant, who has some inflated ideas of his own, and lacks the requisite wisdom to understand what he is about to get himself into, unwittingly replaces the secret word into the amulet and brings the Golem back to life during the Rabbi's absence.

The assistant is in love with the Rabbi's daughter, who in turn, is having a secret affair with a Christian knight against the expressed instructions not to by her father. The assistant is hoping to use the Golem's strength against his rival to win the hand of the Rabbi's daughter. He is unable, however, to control the Golem, who subsequently goes on a rampage.

Once operating out of the parameters of what he was specifically created for, the Golem is at risk, not because of any inclination toward malice or ill will, but simply because he doesn't know any better. He is ill-equipped to take on and to manage the more subtle and convoluted intrigues of human interaction. The Rabbi's assistant, like the Sorcerer's Apprentice in the movie Fantasia, has exceeded his limits of competency and this sets the stage for tragedy and havoc.

MEYRINK'S GOLEM

Meyrink's story of the Golem takes place during the fin de siècle of the 18th and 19th centuries. You can feel the throbbing of humanity in the narrow streets of Prague. There's the holy man Schemajah Hillel and his dutiful daughter Miriam; the Miser Aaron Wasserman, and his inflated son, who has been protected from life by his father until he "literally reveled in the idea of himself as the arch physician, appointed to pronounce upon the weal and woe of his fellow creatures." (Meyrink, 20)

Other characters include the red headed Rosina, the whore, Charousek the medical student, and Zottman the murderer. There are also the insensitive bureaucrats and the charitable Dr. Hulbert, betrayed by his younger wife. And of course, there is the main character, Pernath, the repairer of fine books and jewelry, who seems content to stay to himself until he is literally pulled into the fray by things beyond his control. And the common denominator for the entire story, is the legion of the Golem.

Meyrink begins his tale with the main character Pernath, reflecting to himself. Pernath has had a vague notion of unrest in his soul in recent days. He has been reading from the writings of the Buddha, and a certain passage has been ruminating in his mind from a recent dream. The passage (Meyrink, 1976) is as follows:

> A crow flew down to a stone that looked, as it lay, like a lump of fat. Thought the crow, 'Here is a toothsome morsel for my dinning,' but finding it nothing of the kind, away it flew again. So do we crows, having drawn near to the stone, even so do we, would be seekers after truth, abandon Gautama the Ascetic so soon as in him we cease to find pleasure. (1)

Shortly thereafter, a stranger brings a certain book to Pernath for repair. A section of this book, entitled the *Foundation of the Soul*, or *Ibbur*, has a large beginning letter I, that has been worn away. The letter's design is unique and makes its presence known in Janus like fashion by appearing on opposite sides of the adjoining pages, a juxtaposition. As Pernath studies the book it reminds him of his dream about the crow and the stone. In shifting through the pages of the book he comes upon the following description which captures his attention.

> A throng of Corybantes came rushing out of the distance. A man and a woman were embracing. I saw them from afar, and nearer and nearer came the throng. Now I heard the singing of the frenzied troop close to me, and my eyes sought out the embracing couple. But they turned into a single form, half male, half female—a hermaphrodite seated on a throne of mother-of-pearl. Its crown terminated in a piece of red wood, on which a Worm of Destruction had gnawed mysterious runic figures. Pattering blindly behind came the flock of

miniature sheep, in a cloud of dust—perambulating proven-
der that the giant hermaphrodite trailed in its wake to feed its
train of dancing bacchantes. (11-12)

Heretofore unknown parts of Pernath start to stir from within—
and he begins to develop his feeling function, which is uncharac-
teristic of him. He gets more deeply in touch with who he is and
begins to fall in love with Miriam, which ironically, is also the
name of Rabbi Loew's daughter from one of the earlier stories.
His superior (thinking) and auxiliary (sensate) functions are being
augmented and supplemented by the heretofore second auxiliary
(intuition) and inferior (feeling) functions.

Furthermore, all the characters in the story, like parts of a
dream, are really all different parts of Pernath. Each part needs
to be integrated into the whole to achieve the resurrected "I"
(the repair of the book) and to foster the state of individuation.
If the characters remain distinct and in opposition, integration
will remain on the proverbial backburner, and Pernath too, will
lose interest in the pursuit of the larger truth. The pleasure he
currently feels will begin to dissipate (smaller *coniunctio*). With
this dissipation all heretofore projections will be maintained.

MYSTERIOUS WAYS

Like God, the unconscious can work in mysterious ways. Pernath,
is accused of murdering the miser, and is locked away to languish
in a prison cell. This experience is what might be imagined as
his 'dark night of the soul'—his decent into the underworld or
unconscious. The cell or container in which he is housed begins
to loosen the grip of Pernath's ego and its insistence in following

a habitual way of seeing and defining things. This results in the development of a functioning Ego-Self Axis within the confines of the prison cell (Pernath's interior) and promotes an interface between thinking, sensation, intuition, and feeling.

CONCLUSIONS

The figure of the Golem symbolizes the process of individuation and transcendence. It symbolizes the creation of something new. But to create something new first requires more than just the run-of-the-mill inflated desire to succeed. It requires dedication and humility. With human beings, one of these conditions is usually absent, because as a species humans are wired to take the path of least resistance. They prefer to latch onto easy solutions. Jung once stated that "Nothing is more dangerous than a superficial understanding of everything (CW 16, ¶197). Humans are drawn to easy solutions because they offer a sense of safety while quickly reducing anxiety.

The process of individuation, however, requires a deep understanding of one's own limitations as well as the ability to maintain a great respect for the powers of the unconscious (Self/God). Matthew stated:

> Enter through the narrow gate; for the gate is wide and the road is easy that leads to destruction, and there are many who take it. For the gate is narrow and the road is hard that leads to life, and there are few who find it. (Matthew 7:13-14, *Bible* *New Revised Standard Version*).

CHAPTER 12

DORIAN GRAY

Persona, Shadow, and the Deep Archetypal Dark

PCL-R score = 22 (Suspicious range)

He who kills his conscious conscience?, kills himself.

—ANDRE MAUROIS

I turned halfway around and saw Dorian Gray for the first time. When our eyes met, I felt that I was growing pale. A curious sensation of terror came over me. I knew I had come face to face with someone whose mere personality was so fascinating that, if I allowed it to do so, it would absorb my whole nature, my whole soul, my very art itself.

—OSCAR WILDE, *A Picture of Dorian Gray*

THIS STATEMENT FROM OSCAR Wilde's *A Picture of Dorian Gray* represents a threshold, of sorts, where one can be seduced to cross or, if more fortunate, to find the wherewithal to resist.

The results of a bad choice can be most tragic, and Basil Hallward, the person behind the quote, stands on such a threshold. The dramatics involved can provide both a foreboding sense that aids one's resistance, or a more seductive coloring that usurps one's better judgment. The outcome is always 'to be determined.'

The situation described reminds me of four other instances previously mentioned in this book. The first instance involved my personal account of meeting an individual who exercised a strange hypnotic effect over me—one I attributed to some malevolent force related to the devil.

The second two manifestations occurred in Stevenson's book *The Strange Case of Dr. Jekyll and Mr. Hyde* and categorized Enfield's and Utterson's initial encounters with Hyde. Both reported feeling as if they had come into the presence of some energy related to Satan, a presence that made the hair on their backs stand up. The fourth was the hypnotic music played by the Pied Piper.

As I have already suggested, however, in the chapter on Dr. Jekyll and Hyde, Hyde is not a representation of a personal shadow complex like most of the others, but instead a foreboding telltale sign of the archetypal shadow, another name for the devil or Satan, in some traditions.

I know that this will cause consternation in some readers, but I believe that there are forces, unseen, not unlike the gravitational pull of the moon, that influence us beyond our capability to comprehend or manage them. And we need to be conscious of these forces if we are to have a fighting chance in our relationship to them. In previous time periods such phenomenon might be called possession by a demon. Today we might describe it as being under the sway of a complex or acting on an irresistible impulse. Flip Wilson, the comedic actor used to say: "The devil made me do it."

BEGINNING

We begin our present tale in the art studio of Basil Hallward. He is painting a picture of a young, handsome man, by the name of Dorian Gray. Basil, an aficionado of beauty and of the fine arts, is taken in by, and mesmerized by, Dorian's physical perfection. Basil feels privileged and energized to be in the presence of such natural beauty. His association with Dorian feels like a blessed happening—with each party fulfilling fully his half of a dyad, that represents the ideal marriage between painter and subject. All appears idyllic in this scenario until the arrival of Lord Henry.

Lord Henry is an iconoclast. He loves to play the devil's advocate. He is always turning conventional wisdom on its head and seems to be carefree and untethered by morality. On any given day while philosophizing he might state such things as "I choose my friends for their good looks, my acquaintances for their good characters, and my enemies for their good intellects," (11), or "... the bravest man among us is afraid of himself."

The mutilation of the savage has its tragic survival in the self-denial that mars our lives. We are punished for our refusals. Every impulse that we strive to strangle broods in the mind and poisons us." (24), or "Nothing can cure the soul but the senses, just as nothing can cure the senses but the soul." (26) Lord Henry makes such statements easily and with a sense of profound alacrity. He is amused by the reactions of others— who are bruised by his perceived insensitivity. Due to the shock value of his statements, most, if not all, are not facile enough to respond in a timely manner to challenge him successfully. Lord Henry, at the same time, only half understands both himself, and the full implications of what he has said. He prefers effect and startle instead of the comprehension, and can flit easily to the next unsettling remark, enjoying the uncomfortable state he has invoked in others. He is a man with vast knowledge, yet he lacks dept and wisdom. Wisdom or depth would not allow for such audacious non-sense. He has a meager concept of integration. While he seems to recognize the polarity of sense and soul, he has no idea of how to bring them together. He sees this dilemma as a mystery. Lord Henry states:

> Soul and body, body, and soul—how mysterious they were! There is animalism in the soul, and the body has its moments of spirituality. The senses could refine, and the intellect could degrade. Who could say where the fleshy impulse ceased, or the psychical impulse began? How shallow were the arbitrary definitions of ordinary psychologists! And yet how difficult to decide between the claims of the various schools! Was the soul a shadow seated in the house of sin? Or was the body really in the soul, as Giordano Bruno thought? The separation of spirit from matter was a mystery, and the union of spirit with matter was also a mystery. (72-73)

During his first chance meeting with Dorian, which Basil Hallward has attempted to prevent, Lord Henry observes the lovely connection between Basil and Dorian. He becomes jealous and instantly embraces the intent of disrupting this current stable exchange to claim Dorian for himself. Although Basil is supposedly one of his friends, Lord Henry, who is a thinking type, doesn't much care about upsetting the sensitivities of others, especially if they stand in the way of his gratifying one of his senses. To achieve his selfish desires, Lord Henry will adroitly assume a calculating, psychopathic, Iago-like strategy (Shakespeare, Othello) to achieve his impulsive, titillating aims. Dorian and Basil, for all intents and purposes, become Desdemona and Othello. Lord Henry looks for and experiments with ways to influence Dorian. He accomplishes this by appealing to his Dorian's baser instincts. Dorian, who is prime and proper, naïve, and apparently pure and un-blemished, is woefully unprepared to deal with such temptations. He is well positioned to fulfill one of Oscar Wide's numerous witticisms, namely 'the only thing I cannot resist is temptation.' Lord Henry begins his seduction of Dorian with an attack on a place where most human beings are vulnerable—their fear of death and with the process of growing old. Lord Henry turns and looks at the finished portrait of Dorian, resting leisurely on the easel, in all its glory, and states:

You have only a few years in which to live really, perfectly, fully. When your youth goes, your beauty will go with it, and then you will suddenly discover that there are no triumphs left for you or have to content yourself with those mean triumphs that the memory of your past will make more bitter than defeats. Every month brings you nearer to something dreadful. Time is jealous of you, and wars against your lilies and your roses. You will become sallow, and hollow cheeked, and dull-eyed. (28)

Dorian, listening to Lord Henry, reflects to himself:

Yes, there would be a day when his face would be wrinkled and wizen, his eyes dim and colorless, the grace of his figure broken and deformed. The scarlet would pass away from his lips, and the gold steal from his hair. The life that was to make his soul would mar his body. He would become dreadful, hideous, and uncouth. (32)

Dorian then speaks out loud about his reflections

How sad it is! I shall grow old, and horrible, and dreadful. But this picture will remain always young. It will never be older than this particular day in June.... If it were only the other way! If it were I that was to be always young, and the picture that was to grow old! For that—for that—I would give everything! Yes, there is nothing in the whole world I would not give! I would give my soul for that. (32-33)

DORIAN'S FIRST OFFENSE

Dorian becomes fascinated by Lord Henry's philosophy of life. At one point in the story Lord Henry says to Dorian: "Yes, Dorian, you will always be fond of me. I represent to you all the sins you have never had the courage to commit." (100) Dorian, as a result, begins to feed his senses. He is enthralled by all that life has to offer, especially after all restraints have been dismantled.

One night, by chance, Dorian happens by a small theater, well removed from the more famous and reputable marquess. He is coaxed by the owner, barking to passersby, to attend the show. Once inside Dorian is mesmerized by a young actress by the name of Sibyl Vane. Sibyl is beautiful and gives herself totally

---

Portrait of Dorian Gray as a Young Man

over to the characters she plays on the stage—heroines such as Juliet, Imogen, Rosalind, and Desdemona. Although the productions and surroundings are shabby and second rate, Sibyl gives an authentic measure to each role that she plays. These characters, however, are her assumed personas, who are apparently much more interesting than who she is in actual life. Sibyl lives modestly at home with her mother, and they both subsist off the modest income from Sibyl's acting. Sibyl's father, an aristocrat who had impregnated Sibyl's mother, abandoned her and reneged on any responsibilities. Dorian, enthralled by Sibyl's personas, knows nothing of Sibyl's humble roots and projects onto her his ideal of the perfect woman—the same characteristics that perfectly align themselves with the heroic characters embodied on the stage. As a result, Dorian only knows Sybil as the heroine, and Sibyl unfortunately only knows Dorian as Prince Charming—a projection of her own longing and desires. They are in love with projections—not with one another's real, authentic selves.

When Dorian tells Lord Henry about his love for Siubyl Vane, Lord Henry teases him and states:

> My dear boy, the people who love only once in their lives are really shallow people. What they call loyalty, and their fidelity, I call either the lethargy of custom or their lack of imagination. Faithfulness is to the emotional life what consistency is to the life of the intellect—simply a confession of failure. (62)

Lord Henry then asks Dorian to dine with him but Dorian declines. Dorian states: "Tonight she is Imogen, and tomorrow night she will be Juliet." (68) Lord Henry amused, then asks: "When is she Sibyl Vane ?"(68) Dorian prophetically responds,

"Never." Lord Henry then states: "I congratulate you." (68) It is interesting, to say the least, that Dorian is not even curious about who the real Sibyl is. He is content with maintaining his fantasy about Sibyl because it perfectly parallels his own ideal creation. The above exchange with Lord Henry foretells the tragic events which will occur in short order after Dorian invites his friends to attend one of Sibyl's performances.

Prior to the above-mentioned performance, however, Dorian shares his intent to marry Sibyl with Basil Hallward and Lord Henry. Dorian states to Lord Henry:

I love Sibyl Vane. I want to place her on a pedestal of gold, and to see the world worship the woman who is mine. What is marriage? An irrevocable vow. You mock at it for that. Ah! Don't mock. It is an irrevocable vow that I want to take. Her trust makes me faithful; her belief makes me good. When I am with her, I regret all that you have taught me. I become different from what you have known me to be. I am changed, and the mere touch of Sibyl Vane's hand makes me forget you and all your wrong, fascinating, poisonous, delightful theories. (97-98)

On the night that Dorian has invited his friends Basil Hallward and Lord Henry to attend one of Sibyl's performances there is a major shift in Sibyl. Until this point, she has only shown her persona to Dorian in the form of the heroine. Sibyl, however, is beginning to open her heart. She is beginning to have the courage to become herself because she believes in Dorian's genuine love for her. Thus, she has decided to drop all pretenses, built over time to protect her from the cruel world. She wants to share her true self with Dorian, but in deciding to do so she has lost the desire to act. She wants to be herself with Dorian and not to just embody a shallow persona that appears to have depth. Her performance that night, as a result, is anything but heroic—but what does that matter—Sibyl is in love! She no longer feels the need to escape into fantasy. Love disarms her.

After the show Dorian hurries to see Sibyl back-stage. He is upset and mortified that his friends have attended such a mediocre performance. Upon entering Sibyl's dressing room, instead of finding a despondent actress, Sibyl is smiling and looks at Dorian while stating, almost with a sense of amusement: "How badly I acted tonight, Dorian." (107) Dorian responds by stating: "Horribly! It was dreadful. Are you ill? You have no idea what it was. You have no idea what I suffered." (107) Here Dorian displays his self-centeredness. His ego, ever vulnerable to deflation, has been pricked. His inquiry into Sibyl's possible illness is totally superficial – no deeper than the ubiquitous greeting 'how are you?' He asks this question only to soothe his own embarrassment and shame.

Sibyl, still smiling, attempts to understand Dorian's reaction. She believes that Dorian should have intuitively understood what has happened, and why she has lost her desire to act. In her attempt to explain her bad performance Sybil states:

Dorian, Dorian, before I knew you, acting was the one reality of my life. It was only in the theatre that I lived. I thought that it was all true. I was Rosalind one night, and Portia the other. The joy of Beatrice was my joy, and the sorrows of Cordelia were mine also. I believed in everything. The common people who acted with me seemed to me to be godlike. The painted scenes were my world. I knew nothing but shadows, and I thought them real. You came—oh, my beautiful love! —and freed my soul from prison. You taught me what realty really is. Tonight, for the first time in my life, I saw through the hollowness, the sham, the silliness of the empty pageant in which I had always played. Tonight, for the first time, I became conscious that the Romeo was hideous, and old, and painted, that the moonlight in the orchard was false, that the scenery was vulgar, and that the words I had to speak were unreal, were not my words, were not what I wanted to say. You brought me something higher, something of which all be art is but a reflection. You had made me understand what love really is. My love! My love! Prince Charming! Prince of life. I have grown sick of shadows. You are more to me than art can ever be. What have I to do with puppets of a play? When I came on tonight I could not understand how it was that everything had gone from me. I thought that I was going to be wonderful. I found that I could do nothing. Suddenly it dawned on my soul what it all meant. The knowledge was exquisite to me. I heard them hissing, and I smiled. What could they know of love such as ours? Take me away, Dorian—take me away with you, where we can be quite alone. I hate the stage. I might mimic a passion that I do not feel, but I cannot mimic one that burns like fire. Oh, Dorian, Dorian, you understand now what it signifies? Even if I could do it, it would be profanation for me to play being in love. You have made me see that. (109-110)

Dorian is aghast. He does not understand anything beyond his acute agony that his projections have been shattered. He states:

You have killed my love. You have killed my love. You used to stir my imagination. Now you don't even stir my curiosity. You simply produce no effect. I loved you because you were marvelous, because you had genius and intellect, because you realized the dreams of great poets and gave shape and substance to the shadows of art. You have thrown it all away. You are shallow and stupid. My God! How mad I was to love you. What a fool I have been. You are nothing to me now. I will never see you again. I will never think of you. I will never mention your name. You don't know what you were to me once. Why once... Oh, I can't bear to think of it! I wish I had never laid eyes upon you! You have spoiled the romance of my life. (10)

Dorian leaves Sibyl is a state of shock and despair. With her heart heavy with rejection, much like how her mother must have felt after she too was abandoned, Sibyl poisons herself and dies in her dressing room. Dorian returns home and has no idea that Sibyl has killed herself. As he is passing by the portrait that Basil has painted, he is taken aback by something that he catches out of the corner of his eye. Upon inspection of the portrait Dorian notices that there is a change in his expression. There is the suggestion of cruelty in his mouth. Dorian is taken aback. Might this be an indication that his conscience is being stirred? Will he now be remorseful? He then remembers the words that he spoke about the picture growing old. He recalls clearly that day in Basil's studio and his thoughts at the time. He reflects:

He had uttered a mad wish that he himself might remain young and the portrait grow old; that his own beauty might be untarnished, and the face on the canvas bear the burden of his passions and his sins; that the painted image might be seared with the lines of suffering and thought, and that he might keep all the delicate bloom and loveliness of his just conscious boyhood. (117)

Dorian is momentarily unhinged and anxious. His tranquility has been disturbed and his "just conscious boyhood" lacks the depth of character to handle such a disturbance. He makes use of the psychological defense mechanism 'undoing' when he reflects further, in the statement below, about the change he has noticed in the portrait:

For every sin he committed, a stain would fleck and wreck its fairness. But he would not sin. The picture, changed or unchanged, would be to him the visible emblem of con-science. He would resist temptation. He would not see Lord Henry anymore—would not, at any rate, listen to those subtle, poisonous theories that Basil Hallward's garden had first stirred within him the passion for impossible things. (119)

Dorian then goes to bed and sleeps soundly until late the next morning thinking that he has solved his dilemma. Still unaware of Sibyl's death he wakes up with a sense of restored purpose. Remembering the hint of cruelty on his face in the portrait Dorian sets out to redeem himself. There still appears to be some potential for a rehabilitated self. Dorian recognizes that he has indeed been selfish and wants to make reparations for what he has done. Sibyl can still be his wife and someone to pull him back from the abyss. He decides to compose a letter to Sibyl with "wild words of sorrow, and wilder words of pain." (123) But like the City Counsel in Hamlin this represents a quick pro quo. He makes the decision to repent under duress and not out of a full consciousness of his ever-growing Dark Adaptation which has deep roots.

Lord Henry arrives at Dorian's house and finds Dorian in his state of repentance. Dorian states that he loves Sibyl and that he intends to marry her because "I want to be good. I can't bear the idea of my soul being hideous." (14)

Lord Henry is surprised at Dorian's behavior and asks Dorian "Didn't you get the letter I sent you?" (125)

Dorian says that yes, he had received the letter but "I have not read it yet, Henry. I was afraid there might be something in it that I wouldn't like. You cut life to pieces with your epigrams." (125)

The letter would indeed be something that Dorian wouldn't like. Lord Henry then informs Dorian of Sibyl's death. Dorian is shocked and outlines to Lord Henry the events of the prior evening, including Sibyl's explanation for why she acted poorly. Dorian describes his reaction to Sibyl's outpouring and how he later came to lament his subsequent rejection of Sibyl. Prior to sleep Dorian had settled on his desire to make things right again, and this plan for the morrow had brought him some semblance of peace.

Lord Henry, however, brings up the possibility that a scandal might arise out of this and do harm to Dorian's reputation, which by the way, is already quite suspect by this time. Lord Henry, however, knows nothing about the change in the picture when Dorian states:

I can't tell you what it was (alluding to the change in the portrait), but it was terrible. I said that I would go back to her. I felt that I had done wrong. And now she is dead. My God!

The Changes in the Portrait of Dorian Gray

My God! Harry what shall I do? You don't know the danger that I am in, and there is nothing to keep me straight. She would have done that for me. She had no right to kill herself. It was selfish of her. (127)

Dorian is quickly recovering his composure (persona restoration) by rationalizing that Sibyl is to blame for her own death. He, in turn, is blameless. Dorian is then able to shrug off his brief encounter with pain, worry, and shame so much so that he agrees to join Lord Henry later that night at the opera. The next day Basil Hallward pays Dorian a visit to give his condolences about Sibyl. He is aghast to learn that Dorian had attended the opera the night before. He is taken further aback by Dorian's apparent cold-heartedness toward the death of Sibyl Vane.

He then confronts Dorian about numerous rumors and disheartening vulgar gossip that he has been hearing about his friend, which can't be possibly true. He has believed, up to this moment, that his friend is pure and good natured. Now something has changed. Something just doesn't add up.

Dorian, however, becomes upset with Basil 's accusatory comments, and while not admitting to anything, Dorian starts to realize that his behavior has stirred up a lot of controversy. His behavior has not gone un-noticed. He feels a building agitation about these judgments. He doesn't like the idea that others are paying such close attention to his "personal business." His irritation grows exponentially. He then pivots, looking for a way out of his current dilemma, and finds it. Yes, it is all because of that portrait that Basil has painted! Dorian, in his effort to shift responsibility away from himself, then discloses the secret of the painting to Basil Hallward.

Basil is stricken with fear and horror. He feels a deep empathy for Dorian, but Dorian, thinking only of himself, concludes that Basil is the cause of all his current sufferings. In a wild rage, Dorian picks up a knife which is nearby and kills his friend from behind in cold blood. Not all of Dorian has been entirely consumed by rage, however. He again realizes, at some part of his being, though again too late, that Basil, like Sibyl before him, could have helped him turn his life away from evil. But the chance had been lost. The Dark Adaptation process and the slide toward perdition are well under way. Any wishful thinking on the part of Dorian that any of these dark, foreboding things were not true are quickly dismissed upon a quick inspection of the picture. Dorian reflects:

> It was the living death of his own soul that troubled him. Basil had painted the portrait that had marred his life. He could not forgive him that. It was the portrait that had done everything. Basil had said things to him that were unbearable, and yet he had borne with patience. The murder had been simply the madness of a moment. (283)

Dorian continues to delude himself that all is not lost, despite the fact he continues to perform dastardly deeds. For example, he manipulates, through emotional blackmail, his erstwhile friend Alan Campbell, who subsequently kills himself out of shame. Power over another would continue to be a way for Dorian to assuage his own sense of inadequacy. At another point he meets a woman named Hetty who is about to fall in love with him. He sends her away, ostensibly, so as not to repeat the experience he had with Sybil. He very much wants to find a way to rescue himself—but again his intentions are only superficial. He reflects: "A new life! That is what he wanted. That was what he was waiting for. Surely it had already begun. He had spared one innocent thing, at any rate. He would never again tempt innocence. He would be good." (283) But Dorian was only being good—or his version of good, for selfish purposes. His letting Hetty go was not to prevent her suffering, but more to reverse the noticeable ravages visited upon Basil's painting by his actions. Such reversals never occurred, however, as his behavior was never other than selfish. Dorian would continue to refuse to take any responsibility.

SENSE AND SPIRIT

As Dorian becomes more anxious, he is oftentimes drawn to a particular opium den that offers an instant means to dull his growing shame and guilt. But when Dorian ignores the promptings of the archetypal Self, and its insistence on integration and wholeness, there are mounting consequences. It becomes increasingly difficult for Dorian to just turn away from the psychological rumblings that disturb his waking life and his sleep. He is being charged with the responsibility to solve the mystery of the interplay between sense and spirit. When something is out of balance, and one sided, the psyche will present us with opportunities to address this. Some solutions can result in a growing sense of balance, while others can produce, when cornered, something tragic or destructive.

At one of their subsequent meetings Lord Henry senses something gloomy and miserable in Dorian. He is an expert at finding one's jugular, so he states to Dorian with half closed eyes: "By the way Dorian, what does it profit a man if he gains the whole world and lose—how does the quotation run?—his own soul" (275) Lord Henry is still not consciously aware of the changes in the picture of Dorian Gray, but he senses blood in the water.

After Lord Henry departs, Dorian goes quickly up to the room at the top of the stairs, where the painting is stored. He aggressively drags the purple cloth, which hides the picture, away from the portrait. A cry of pain and anguish erupt from his throat. He can see no change for the better, as he had desperately hoped. Instead, there is only the enlarged look of cunning, and the curved wrinkle of the hypocrite formed on his mouth and lips.

Dorian seizes the same knife that he used to kill Basil Hallward and slashes the portrait, thinking that this will put an end to his suffering. He cries out in agony as he falls to the floor, dying, with a knife through his own heart. Unlike Dr. Jekyll, however, who had sacrificed himself to stop the evil of Hyde, Dorian is simply and selfishly trying to rid himself of the constant reminder of his own immorality and his loss of soul. He intended to kill the portrait – to destroy the evidence. He did not consciously intend to kill himself. Mysteriously the picture is restored to its original pristine beauty.

In the last scene, Wilde describes what the servants saw after breaking down the door to investigate the horrible scream they had heard in the middle of the night:

When they entered, they found hanging upon the wall a splendid portrait of their master as they had last seen him, in all the wonder of his exquisite youth and beauty. Lying on the floor was a dead man, in evening dress, with a knife in his heart. He was withered, wrinkled, and loathsome of visage. It was not until they examined the rings that they recognized who it was. (286-287)

CHAPTER 13

SUMMARY AND REFLECTIONS

To the reader, thank you for your time and attention. Although continuing to be a work in progress, I have worked to develop a growing objective understanding of "the other person's" worldview while constantly reminding myself not to project my own issues onto the people I evaluate, nor to assume that everyone thinks as I do.

I have reflected deeply on the ideas presented here within, such as archetypes, complexes, psychological allergies, Dark Adaptation, Free Will, and Good and Evil. I will continue to delve into additional areas where-ever my curiosity leads me.

In this book I have explored the psychological underpinnings of several recognizable monsters from classical literature who represent prototypal figures who characteristics will inevitably manifest in the lives of real individuals. I have explored the nature of violence and underscored some differences between individuals with occasional lapses in judgment, those with antisocial tendencies, and those who are entirely dark adapted and afflicted with full-fledged Psychopathy. The reader was also introduced to several psychological instruments that help to measure levels of psychopathy. I have underscored the fact that all people do not operate with the same level of intellect, emotional control, forethought, or concern for possible consequences, and that we should keep this in mind when we are casting dispersions or making judgments.

Our ability to differentiate between the differences in individuals is an important one because it will aid us in our decision—making process about who will benefit from treatment, who is ready for parole or probation, or who should be humanely contained and never released from behind the walls of containment. These decisions are best rendered by a team working together and not by any one individual working in isolation. Teamwork is what keeps us humbly tethered to reality and less subject to inflation. I believe that this model is one that will also work in other areas beyond the forensic/psychological terrain.

I have provided tools for the psychological evaluation of dangerous individuals and believe that these tools can serve both the professional as well as the lay person in having a better idea of the nature and forces that we are up against in assuming such responsibilities. The concept of 'Dark or Light Adaptation', since everything is bi-polar in the sense that in wholeness there are always two poles that constitute an event or experience, reinforces the idea that an individual, all things being equal, will act according to the dictates of his or her nature, a nature that has been formed over time and has now become largely habitual.

There is habit and there is *habitus*. When acting out of habit a prosocial person will gravitate towards being a law-abiding citizen, whereas the antisocial individual will likely run afoul of the law at some point and find themselves in trouble, legal, personal, or otherwise. Accordingly, the more antisocial or psychopathic an individual, the darker adapted, and the less amenable the person is to therapeutic rehabilitation.

You may recall that I introduced the Psychopathy Checklist as a tool that asks the professional to consider a variety of indicators that a person may have a psychopathic personality. A decision that would affect an individual's access to rehabilitation and therapy would never be made on the basis of a simple checklist. From my own story, you can see that many years of training and experience working with those convicted of crimes, under the direction of more seasoned professionals, is required before one is entrusted with the responsibility for a final decision, always done in consultation with others.

Given the nature of the psychopathic personality, a person is skilled in sensing what the interviewer wants and in adapting convincing emotional demonstrations of remorse and empathy. As I pointed out, psychopaths may actually use therapy not to change but rather to become better at feigning emotional traits of caring and empathy by observing the therapist.

That being said, let's take a look at the scores on Psychopathy Check List-Revised (PCL-R) I have given to the "Monsters" in this book. Mr. Hyde and Dracula are the only ones operating in the designated psychopathic range of criminal behavior, with

Psychopathy Check List-Revised

Mr. Hyde	33	Frankenstein	7
Dracula	32	Dr. Jekyll	4
Dorian Gray	22	Pied Piper	4
Phantom	16	Creature	3
Werewolf	12	Golem	3

scores of 33 and 32, respectively. This clearly differentiates them from the others. Dorian Gray falls in the suspicious range at 22. The Phantom and Werewolf would both qualify for a diagnosis of very mild "antisocial personality disorder." (DSM 301.7), while it could be argued that the others demonstrate some tendencies and characteristics of Adult Antisocial Behavior (V71.01), a diagnosis that doesn't require a long history of problematic behavior beginning in childhood. But if you are not a psychopath you have the potential for redemption and the possibility to still turn your life into something that is valued by your own sense of self and by the collective.

As stated previously, antisocial individuals make up a large percentage of the prison population. Unlike psychopaths, they can theoretically and practically derive benefit from psychological treatments and educational opportunities, which will strengthen pro-social connections while weakening the reinforcement of their antisocial inclinations. These efforts are worthwhile and should be supported. They contribute to the betterment of humankind.

My thoughts return to what I have learned from the "monsters" of myth and fiction, which can often teach us more about the dark side of the human psyche than textbooks. These stories may help to protect us from acting on our own darker inclinations or being naive about the existence of the dark side in others.

I have a picture in my consulting room entitled "The All-World Monster Map," which I purchased many years ago at the Chicago Field Museum of Natural History (pp. 250-251). In looking it over I realize that I have only covered, in this current book, a small portion of the mythological creatures from around the world who have disturbed our human slumber. I also realize, with some surprise, that all the monsters that I have researched and focused on have been masculine.

In my next book I hope to write about some of the feminine monsters left out of my initial inquiry including the Selkie Mermaids of Ireland, the Slavic Rusalka, the Succubus, the Medusa, and the *Vagina dentata* or *Ainu*. I am already excited about the work ahead.

Chief Dreadwood
Canadian Pacific Coast

Grim Reaper
Underground Location
He'll Find You

Frost Giant
Jotunheim

OMNIS
MUNDA
TABUL
GEOGRAPH
MONSTRO

Bigfoot
Washington

Banshee
Ireland

Mermaids
North Atlantic

Morlocks
Underworld

Casino Head
Las Vegas

Headless Horseman
Sleepy Hollow

Werev
France

Quetzalcoatl
Mexico

Zombies
Haiti

Missing Monster
Bermuda Triangle

Sirens
Antiquity

Anans
West Africa

Incubus
Nightmares

Freak Daddy
Rain Forest

Sea Serpent
Tropic of Capricorn

Creature from the Black Lagoon
Amazon

Great Beast of the Apocalypse and the Four Horsemen
Imperil Entire Earth

International Monster Commission
These Monsters have been duly certified All-World by the International Monster Commission
1999

Big Stick, Inc.
509 Aurora Avenue #609
Naperville, IL 60540 USA
Tel 1-800-335-7845
BigStickInc.com

"Monster Map" (Devanne, 2000)

BIBLIOGRAPHY

Abraham, K. (1927) Character-formation on the genital level of the libido. In Karl Abraham, *Selected papers on psychoanalysis*. Hogarth Press; London.

Aichorn, A. (1925) *Wayward youth*. Viking Books; New York.

Alexander, F. (1930) *Psychoanalysis and the total personality*. Nervous and Mental Disease Publications; New York.

Alter, R. (2019) *The Hebrew Bible*. Vol. 1. W.W. Norton & Company, New York, and London.

Anonymous. (1957) *Beowulf*. Penguin Classics. Middlesex, England.

APA Ethical Principles of Psychologists and Code of Conduct. 1992. American Psychological Association: 750 First Street, Washington, D.C. 20002-4242.

An American Werewolf in Paris. (1997) A film by Anthony Waller. Hollywood Pictures.

Arieti, Silvano. (1967) *The Intrapsychic Self: Feeling, Cognition, and Creativity in Health and Mental Illness*. Basic Books, Inc. New York, and London.

Aristotle. (1925) *The Nicomachean Ethics*. Oxford University Press, Oxford.

Athens, L. (1992) *The Creation of Violent Dangerous Criminals*. University of Illinois Press. Urbana and Chicago.

Baumeister, R.F. 1997. *Evil: Inside Human Violence and Cruelty*. W. H. Freeman & Company; New York.

Becker, E. (1973) *The Denial of Death*. Simon & Schuster; New York.

Bloch, Chayim. (1925) *Golem: Legends of the Ghetto of Prague*. Kessinger Publishing

Borden, W. (2009) *Contemporary Psychodynamic Theory and Practice*. Lyceum Books; Chicago.

Bowlby, J. (1973) *Separation, Anxiety and Anger*. Basic Book, Inc.; New York.

Browning, R. (1993) *The Pied Piper of Hamelin*. Random House, New York.

Cleckley, H. (1941) *The Mask of Sanity*. 5th edt. Emily S. Cleckley Publishers; 3024 Fox Spring Road, Augusta, Georgia, 30903.

Cotterell, A. & Storm, R. (2003) *The Ultimate Encyclopedia of Mythology*. Hermes House Publishing; London.

Curse of the Werewolf. (1961) A movie directed by Anthony Dawson.

Diagnostic and Statistical Manual of Mental Disorders. (2013) 5th edition. American Psychiatric Publishing. Washington, D.C., London, England.

Dickens, Charles. (1981) *A Tale of Two Cities*. Easton Press, Norwalk, Connecticut.

Du Bois, W.E.B. (1905) *The Souls of Black Folk*, Chapter 12.

Early, E. (1983) A Review of Dr. Jekyll and Mr. Hyde. *The San Francisco Jung Institute Library Journal*; San Francisco.

Eisler, R. (1995) *The Chalice and the Blade: Our History, Our Future*. Harper One, New York.

Freud, S. (1916) *Some character types met with in psychoanalytic work*. Standard Edition 14:309-333. Hogarth Press; London.

Frost, B. (2003). *The Essential Guide to Werewolf Literature*. Popular Press; Madison, WI.

Game of Thrones. Home Box Office Hit Television Show. Season 2.

Grimm's Fairy Tales. (1993) *The Spirit in the Bottle*. Barnes & Noble Publishing, Inc.

Goethe. (1990) *Faust*. (Translated and with an introduction by Walter Kaufman) Anchor Books; New York.

Golem, The. (1920) Timeless Video, Inc.; North Hollywood, CA

Goodheart, W.B. (1980) Theory of Analytical Interaction. *The San Francisco Jung Institute Library Journal*, Vol. 1, No.4.

Good Will Hunting. (1997) A movie directed by Gus Van Sant

Hare, R. 1993. *Without Conscience: The Disturbing World of the Psychopaths among us.* Pocket Books; New York.

Hare, R. 1991. *The Psychopathy Checklist-Revised.* Multi-Health Systems, Inc.; North Tonawanda, New York.

— —1985a. *The Psychopathy Checklist.* Unpublished manuscript, University of British Columbia; Vancouver, Canada.

— —1970. *Psychopathy: Theory and Research.* Wiley Books; New York.

— — & McPherson, L. M. (1984a) Psychopathy and perceptual asymmetry during verbal dichotic listening.

John, E. & Taupin, B. (1972) Mona Lisa and Mad Hatters. Song on record album Honky Chateau. 1972.

Author, Name of Article, *Journal of Abnormal Psychology.* 93. 141-149.

Hillman, J. (1979) *The Dream and the Underworld.* Harper & Row; New York.

— — (1999) *The Force of Character and the Lasting Life.* Random House; New York.

Hopcke, R. (1999) *A Guided Tour of the Collected Works of C.G. Jung.* Shambhala Books; Boston and London.

Horney, K. (1945) *Our inner conflicts.* Norton Books; New York.

Jacobi, J. (1973) *The Psychology of C. G. Jung.* Yale University Press; New Haven and London.

James, W. (1902) *The Varieties of the Religious Experience.* Folio Society (2008) London.

Johnson, A.M. (1949) Sanctions for superego lacunae of adolescents. In *Searchlights on Delinquency*, ed. K. Eissler, pp. 225- 245. International Universities Press; New York.

Jung, C.G. (1929) *Problems of Modern Psychotherapy*, CW, Vol.16.

— —(1953) *Psychology and Alchemy*, CW, Vol. 12.

— — (1960) *The Structure and Dynamics of the Psyche*. CW Vol. 8

— —(1961) *Memories, Dreams, Reflections*. Random House; New York.

— — (1964) Title of Volueme, CW 10. Princeton, NJ: Princeton University Press.

— — (1967) *Alchemical Studies*. CW Vol. 13.

— — (1973) *The Symbolic Life*. CW, Vol. 18.

— — (1977) *Two Essays on Analytical Psychology*. CW. Vol. 7. Princeton University Press, Princeton, N.J.

— —(1984) *Seminar on Dream Analysis* (1928-1930) Princeton University Press.

— — (1985) *The Practice of Psychotherapy*. CW, Vol. 16.

— — (1989) *The Psychogenesis of Mental Disease*. CW Vol. 3.

— —(1990) *Psychological Types*. CW Vol. 6

Karpman, B. (1941) On the need of setting psychopathy into two distinct clinical types: symptomatic and idiopathic. *Journal of Criminal Psychopathology* 3:112-137.

Kernberg, O. (1984) *Severe Personality Disorders: Psychotherapeutic Strategies*. Yale University Press; New Haven and London.

Klein, M. (1940) Mourning and its relation to manic depressive states. *International Journal of Psychoanalysis*, 21, 125-153.

Larkin, E. (2003) *The Devil in the White City*. Crown Publishers; New York.

Leivick, H. (2001) *The Golem*. Dramatists Play Service, Inc. New York.

Leroux, Gaston. (2006) *The Phantom of the Opera*. Easton Press. Norwalk, Connecticut.

Lilienfeld, Scott & Widows, Michelle R, (2005) Psychopathy Personality Inventory—Revised (PPI-R) Manuel. PAR Publishing. Lutz, Florida

Maudsley, H, (1874), *Responsibility in mental disease.* King Press; London.

Meloy, J.R. (2000) *Violence Risk and Threat Assessment· Specialized Training Services*; San Diego, California

— — (1995) Antisocial Personality Disorder. In G. Gabbard, ed., *Treatments of Psychiatric Disorders*, 2nd. edition. American Psychiatric Press; Washington, D.C.

Meloy, R. (1988) *The Psychopathic Mind: Origins· Dynamics· and Treatment.* Aronson Books; Northvale, New Jersey.

Meyrink, G. (1976) *The Golem.* Dover Publications; New York.

Mills, J. S. (1859) *On Liberty.* Chapter 3.

Milton, J. (2004) *Paradise Lost.* W. W. Norton & Company; New York.

Montague, S. (1991) *The Vampire.* Dorset Press; New York.

Neumann, E. (1990) *Depth Psychology and a New Ethic.* Shambhala Publications, Inc.; Boston.

Newton, Isaac. (1676) Correspondence of Isaac Newton, Vol. 1, 1959, 416.

Nosferatu, the Movie. (1979) A Film by Werner Herzog.

O'Donnell, E. (1996) *Werewolves.* Oracle Publishing; London.

Ouspensky, P.D. (1949) *In Search of the Miraculous: The Teachings of G. I. Gurdjieff.* Harcourt, Inc.; New York.

— —(1974) *The Psychology of Man's Possible Evolution.* Vintage Books; New York.

Paris, G. (2007) *Wisdom of the Psyche: Depth Psychology after neuroscience.* Routledge Books; London/New York

Perera, S. B. (1986) *The Scapegoat Complex: Toward a Mythology of Shadow and Guilt.* Inner City Books. Toronto, Canada.

Pinel, P. (1801) *Traite medico‑philosophique sur l'alienation mentale.* Richard, Calle et Ravier; Paris.

Plato's *Phaedo* (470-399 BC) Sections 62-690.

Plato (2010 / circa 380 BC): *The Allegory of the Cave*. P & L Publications; Monee, Illinois.

Rhodes, R. (1999) *Why they kill: The Discoveries of a Maverick Criminologist*. Vintage Books; New York.

Rice, H.M. & Cormier, C. (1992) Evaluation of a maximum-security therapeutic community for psychopaths and other mentally disordered offenders. *Law and Human Behavior*, 16:399-412.

Roshomon (1950) A movie directed by Kurosawa, Akiro.

Rychlak, J.F. (1981) *Introduction to Personality and Psychotherapy* (2nd. Edition) Houghton Mifflin Company; Boston.

Samuels, A., Shorter, B., & Plaut, F. (2000) *A Critical Dictionary of Jungian Analysis*. Brunner-Routledge; New York.

Santayana, G. (1905) *The Life of Reason* Vol. 1, Chapter 12.

Shakespeare. (1980) *Hamlet: The Tragedies*. Easton Press, Norwich, Connecticut.

Shakespeare. (1980) *Othello*. Easton Press, Norwich, Connecticut.

Shelly, M. (1818/1992) *Frankenstein*. Borzoi Books; New York.

Singer, Isaac Bashevis (1982) *The Golem*. Farrar Straus Giroux, New York.

Snyder, Zack (2007) Warner Brothers Pictures.

Steiger, B. (1999) *The Werewolf Book: The Encyclopedia of Shape-Shifting Being*. Visible Ink Publishers; Detroit/London.

Steinbeck, John. (1994) *Of mice and men*. Penguin Books, USA, Inc.

Stevenson, R.L. (1886) *The Strange Case of Dr Jekyll and Mr Hyde*. The Easton Press. Norwalk, Connecticut.

Stevenson, R. L. (2008) *Olalla*. AEgypan Press; New York.

Stoker, B. (1897/2005) *Dracula*. Easton Press; Norwalk, Connecticut.

Storm, L. (2008) *Synchronicity: Multiple Perspectives on Meaningful Coincidence*. Pari Publishing; Grosseto, Italy.

Summers, M. (1991) *The Vampire*. Dorsett Press; New York.

Terence. (1992) *The Oxford Dictionary of Quotations*. The Easton Press, Norwalk, Connecticut.

The Book of Symbols. (2010) Editor and Chief: Ami Ronnberg. Taschen Publishing. Cologne, Germany

The Herder Dictionary of Symbols. (1986/1993) Edited by Boris Matthews. Chiron Publications, Wilmette, Illinois.

The New English Bible with the Apocrypha. (1970) Oxford University Press, New York.

Thoresen, Are. (2018) *Demons and healing: The Reality of the Demonic Threat and the Doppelganger in the Light of Anthroposophy*. Temple Lodge Publishing. Forest Row, RH18, 5ES.

Van De Graaf, K.M. & Stuart, I.F. (1988) *Concepts of Human Anatomy and Physiology*. 2nd. Edition. Wm. C. Brown Publishers; Dubuque, Iowa.

Venables, H. (1980) *The Frankenstein Diaries*. Viking Press, New York.

Von Franz, M. L. (1996) *The Interpretation of Fairy Tales·* Shambhala. Boston and London.

Wallin, D. (2007) *Attachment in Psychotherapy*. The Guilford Press; New York.

Webster's New World Dictionary of the American Language (1982)

Wegener, Paul. (1920) The Golem (B&W movie)

White, R. B. & Gilliland, R.M. (1975) *Elements of Psychopathology: The Mechanisms of Defense*. Grune & Stratton; New York, San Francisco, and London.

Wiesel, Elie. (1983) *The Golem·* Summit Books, New York.

Wilhelm, Richard. (1931) *The Secret of the Golden Flower*. Harcourt Brace & Company. New York.

Wilde, Oscar (2004) *The Picture of Dorian Gray*. Easton Press, Norwich, Connecticut.

Zipes, J. (1989) *Beauty and the Beast and other Classic French Fairy Tales*. Signet Classic; New York.

Acknowledgments

To complete most projects, especially the arduous work of writing a book, a person needs inexhaustible amounts of encouragement, support, along with a constant flow of constructive feedback. I am the fortunate recipient of all these requirements.

To my friends and colleagues who have listened to and supported me, I give a hearty thanks. Foremost among such a long and august group include John Giannini, George Hogenson, Vlado Solc, Kennon McKee, William Alexi, and Ken James.

In addition, my dear wife Karen Ann deserves my thanks for being my life partner and understanding, perhaps intuitively, my need to reflect, experiment, and make and learn from life's mistakes.

Finally, and not in any way less deserving of my gratitude, I wish to thank Dyane Sherwood, my editor and colleague, who perhaps more than anyone else, made the work possible, and the completion a foregone certainty.

Credits

Cover: Hieronymus Bosch (1450 - 1516), "Visions of the Afterlife," 1490. By permission of Palazzo Ducale, Venice.

"All World Monster Map," 2000. Christopher Devane. By Permission of CHANNEL ETERNITY (TM) channeleternity@gmail.com.

All other illustrations were prepared by Dijana Granov, dijanagranov@gmail.com.

About the Author

PETER DEMUTH began working in the field of psychology at age 21 as an extern at the Sheppard-Pratt Hospital in Baltimore (1975) and subsequently worked his way up the ladder at a local psychiatric hospital, first as a psychiatric nursing aid and then as a unit counselor. During that time, he became very adept at working with the

(Photograph: Mary Henebry, 2022)

chronically mental ill and developed an ability to handle and restrain violent individuals with both respect and empathy.

For a time, Dr. Demuth lived in New York (1980-1982), where he worked as a therapist/mentor for first time youthful offenders in Queens and then as a counselor for inner city youth at the Henry Street Settlement on the lower east side of Manhattan. While living in New York he also pursued an alternate career track in music. He has always felt motivated to write and perform his original folk-pop music, and he continues to do so to the present time.

After leaving New York and spending a winter in Key West playing music, Demuth returned to Baltimore to attend graduate school. To fund his academic studies, he worked as a research recruiter and psychometrician for the Addiction Research Center of the National Institute on Drug Abuse (NIDA) under the direction of Drs. Heartzen and Hickey. In 1985 he was accepted for advanced graduate work in Chicago. During his studies, he worked part time directing a homeless shelter in Wrigleyville and as a Counselor on the psychiatric unit at Saint Joseph Hospital.

After receiving his doctorate in Clinical Psychology from the Illinois School of Professional Psychology (1990), and his master's in Psychology from Loyola University (1985), he further pursued his keen interest in forensics by accepting a job at a maximum-security prison in Maryland as a psychologist tasked with evaluating and treating the inmates assigned to his clinical team. He was also asked to develop and oversee a substance abuse program for individuals whose crimes revolved around securing money to pay for their addictions. Once a week he was also a group therapist for the Sexual Violent Offenders Clinic at the University of Maryland.

In 1998 Dr Demuth returned to Chicago to work as the assistant chief of Psychology and the Director of Clinical Training at the Elgin Mental Health Center. He was promoted to Chief Forensic Psychologist in 2002.

In 2005 Dr. Demuth left the Elgin Mental Health Center to pursue full-time private practice, and in 2012 he earned his Diplomate in Analytical Psychology from the C. G. Jung Institute of Chicago.

At the present time Dr Demuth is a Forensic Psychologist and Jungian Analyst in private practice in Evanston, Illinois. He is an international lecturer as well as an instructor at the C.G. Jung Institute of Chicago and a member of the Chicago Society of Jungian Analysts. He has published on a variety of subjects, including ego strength, psychopathy, the Criminal Code, Death and Transformation, and the use of early memories in a therapeutic prison setting.

In addition to his clinical work and writings, Demuth continues to write and perform his original introspective folk-pop music. He has eight full length albums in circulation and performs regularly in the Chicago area. He lives with his wife Karen, along with their two cats and a golden retriever. They have a son about to graduate from Western Michigan University with hopes to pursue a job in Sports Marketing.